SMART
English Grammar
for Speaking & Writing

2권

SMART English Grammar
for Speaking & Writing 2권

2025년 01월 02일 인쇄
2025년 01월 10일 발행

지 은 이 E & C
발 행 인 Chris Suh
발 행 처 **MENTORS**
경기도 성남시 분당구 황새울로 335번길 10 598
TEL 031-604-0025 FAX 031-696-5221
mentors.co.kr
blog.naver.com/mentorsbook
* Play 스토어 및 App 스토어에서 '멘토스북' 검색해 어플다운받기!
등록일자 2005년 7월 27일
등록번호 제 2009-000027호
I S B N 979-11-94467-26-7
         979-11-94467-24-3(세트)
가   격 18,000원(정답 및 해설 PDF 무료다운로드)

SMART
English Grammar
for Speaking & Writing

2권

▶ 문법이란?

문법이란 문장을 만들어 말을 하고(speaking) 또한 문장을 만드는(writing) 것을 말한다. 모국어를 하는데는 그리 많은 문법이 필요하지 않는다. 어머니 뱃속에서부터 히어링을 하면서 모국어를 익히기 때문에 저절로 알게 되며 나중에 문법의 체계화를 위해 후천적으로 문법을 약간 학습할 뿐이다. 그러나 모국어가 아닌 외국어로 영어를 배우는 과정은 모국어 습득과 정반대가 된다.

▶ 외국어로 영어배우기는…

우리는 영어듣기와 영어말하기에 먼저 노출될 수 없기에 역으로 영문법을 통해서 영어를 말하고 쓰게 되는 과정을 밟아간다. 즉 한 언어, 즉 여기서는 영어를 문법을 통해서 이해하고 이를 발판으로 해서 영어회화, 영어작문 그리고 영어듣기 등에 많은 시간을 쏟고 주구장창 몰두하게 된다. 모국어로 영어를 배우는 네이티브와는 비교될 수 없는 싸움을 하는 것이다. 미국이나 영국에서 네이티브들과 소통하면서 몇년 살면 저절로 배워지는 영어지만 다 그럴 수 없기 때문에 우리는 어쩔 수 없이 비효율적인 방법으로 영어로 익힐 수밖에 없다. 여기에 문법의 중요성이 생기게 된다.

▶ 문법에만 흠뻑 빠지면 안돼…

여기서 한가지 범하기 쉬운 오류가 있다. 문법이 외국어를 배우는 최초의 단계임에는 분명하지만 너무 문법에 사로잡혀서 그래서 완벽한 문장 아니면 말을 하지 못하는 어리석음에 놓일 수가 있다. 언어는 시대에 따라 시시각각 변하고 이를 밑받침하는 문법 역시 계속 변화가 된다. 역으로 생각을 해보자. 우리가 특히 일상생활에서 우리말을 할 때 얼마나 국문법 규칙을 지키면서 말하는지 말이다. 이 말은 문법을 꼭 알아야 하지만 너무 문법에 얽매이면 안된다는 얘기이다.

▶ 이거 알면 남들보다 앞서가…

이 책 <BASIC English Grammar 1권, 2권>과 <SMART English Grammar 1권, 2권>은 지금 시대에 가장 잘 맞는 그리고 꼭 알아야 하는 문법규칙들을 무겁지 않게 정리하여 문법을 공부하는 사람들이 부담스럽지 않게 학습할 수 있도록 꾸며져 있다. 또한 이를 각종 Test들로 확인하게 되어 이를 다 풀고 나면 남들보다는 한두단계 영어에서 앞서 갈 수 있을 것이라 확신한다.

New Grammar is About

1 실용영어를 위한 문법

문법도 실용영어를 하는데 필요한 최소한의 도구이다. 따라서 문법을 위한 문법이 아닌 '실용영어를 위한 문법' 이란 캐치프레이즈를 내걸고 실제로 영어를 읽고 말하는 데 필요한 영어문법 사항들만을 정리하였다. 가장 실용적인 영어회화문(Dialogue)을 통해 우리가 학습해야 할 문법사항을 언급하는 것 또한 '지금,' '현재' 쓰이고 있는 문법을 지향하기 위함이다.

2 영어회화를 위한 문법

실용영어의 목적은 영어로 하는 의사소통이다. '영어말하기' 란 목표를 달성하기 위해 문법에 영어회화를 접목해본다. 문법을 단순한 지식으로 책상에서만 필요한 것이 아니라 실제 영어로 말하는데 활용할 수 있도록 매 Unit별로 학습한 문법지식을 바탕으로 다양한 문장을 영어로 옮겨보는 훈련을 해보며 간접적인 영어회화훈련을 시도해본다. 이는 또한 점점 실용화되고 있는 영어시험자격증인 TOEFL, TOEIC, IELT 등에서 고득점을 취할 수 있는 기본 베이스가 될 수 있을 것이다.

3 다양한 테스트

학습한 문법사항은 연습을 통해 훈련하지 않으면 다 날아가버린다. 이런 과오를 범하지 않기 위해 각 Unit마다 다양한 연습문제를 그리고 각 Chapter가 끝날 때마다 Review Test를 통해 이중으로 테스트를 해보며 머리 속에 오래도록 각인해본다. '영어말하기' 뿐만 아니라 각종 시험에서도 높은 점수를 받을 수 있을 것이다.

Level 2-B
New Grammar is Organized

1 Chapter

시제, 동사류, 명사류 및 수식어류를 학습한 Level 2-A에 이은 Level 2-B에는 동사의 변형, 문장연결하기, 복잡한 구조 이야기 및 주의해야 할 용법 등 총 4개의 Chapter로 구성되어 있다. 먼저 Chapter 5 동사의 변형에서는 문법에서 가장 중요한 부분이라고 해도 과언이 아닌 분사, 수동태, to부정사 및 동명사에 대한 심도있는 학습을 통해 영어문장의 이해를 한층 강화한다. Chapter 6 문장연결하기는 단어, 구, 문장을 이어주는 역할을 하는 전치사와 접속사의 종류와 용법에 대해 정리한다. 다음 Chapter 7 복잡한 구조 이해하기에서는 문장을 길게 만드는 그래서 문장을 어렵게 만드는 명사절, 형용사절, 부사절과 또한 까다로운 부분 중 하나인 가정법 쓰임새를 집중 조명한다. 끝으로 Chapter 8 주의해할 용법에서는 시제일치, 화법, 강조, 도치, 생략 및 부정표현 그리고 문장의 5형식에 대해 친절히 기술함으로써 영어문장의 다양함을 이해해보도록 한다.

총 4개의 Chapters

Chapter 05 | 동사의 변형
분사/ 수동태/ to부정사/ 동명사
Chapter 06 | 문장 연결하기
전치사류/ 접속사류
Chapter 07 | 복잡한 문장구조 이해하기
명사절/ 형용사절/ 부사절/ 가정법
Chapter 08 | 주의해야 할 용법
특수구문/ 문장의 형식

2 Unit

Chapter는 다시 세분되어 각 Chapter별로 7~12개의 Unit로 정리된다. 따라서 총 4개의 Chapter는 총 36개의 Unit로 구성되어 있으며 각 Unit는 다시 Grammar in Practice, Grammar in Use, Unit Test, Writing Pattern Practice 등으로 나누어 진다.

각 Unit의 구성

Grammar in Practice
Grammar in Use
Unit Test
Writing Pattern Practice

3 Review

각 Chapter가 끝날 때마다 Chapter에서 학습한 내용을 다시 복습할 공간을 마련하였다. Review 1, 2에서 종합적으로 문제를 풀어보면서 자신이 학습한 내용을 얼마나 습득하였는지를 확인해볼 수 있다.

4 정답 및 해설

각 Unit의 테스트와 Review의 문제에 대한 정답을 별도의 부록으로 처리하여 문제를 풀 때 정답에 접근하는 것을 어렵게 하여 가급적 스스로 풀어보도록 꾸며졌다.

How to Use this Book

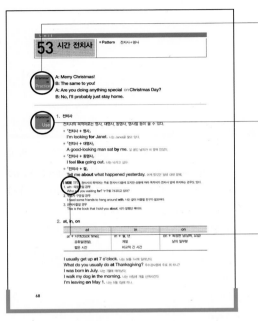

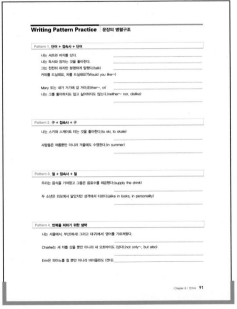

Grammar in Practice

영어회화와 문법을 접목시키는 부분. 각 Unit에서 학습할 문법사항이 실제 영어회화에서는 어떻게 쓰이는지 보면서 문법을 왜 배워야 하는지를 느껴본다.

Grammar in Use

역시 실용성에 focus를 맞춰 불필요한 문법지식을 다 걷어내고 오직 실제로 영어를 말하고 쓰는데 필요한 문법엑기스만을 간단하지만 밀도있게 서술하고 있는 부분이다.

More Tips

Grammar in Use에서 못다한 추가정보를 그때그때마다 간략히 설명해준다.

Unit Test

각 Unit마다 학습한 문법사항을 바로 확인해보는 자리이다. 다양한 형태의 테스트를 통해 학습한 문법지식을 머리 속에 차곡차곡 잊지 않고 기억해둘 수 있다.

Writing Pattern Practice

이번에는 좀 더 적극적으로 문법과 영어회화를 접목시키는 공간이다. 학습한 문법사항을 실제로 영어말하는데 활용해 볼 수 있는 공간으로 문법이 살아있음을 느낄 수 있다.

Review

각 Chapter별로 제공되는 테스트시간으로 일종의 종합문제이다. 이미 Unit Test로 한번 확인한 문법을 다시 한번 꼭꼭 기억할 수 있는 공간이다.

Grammar Point

글로만 읽기에는 복잡한 그러나 중요한 문법사항은 시각적인 표로 다시 한번 정리하여 그 이해를 한층 도왔다.

Contents

* **Chapter 5 동사의 변형**

Unit

41 분사의 역할

● **Pattern** 현재분사: 동사+ing   과거분사: 동사+ed
● **Meaning** 현재분사: ~하고 있는, ~하게 하는   과거분사: ~해진, ~한

A: I'm going abroad on a Working Holiday this summer.
B: Wow! That might be exciting.
A: I'll learn English and get a part-time job.
B: Well, that's killing two birds with one stone.

1. 현재분사와 과거분사

분사란 「동사+ing」 또는 「동사+ed」의 형태로 동사 본래의 성질을 가지고 있으면서 문장 안에서 본동사 또는 형용사 역할을 하는 것을 말한다.

	현재분사	과거분사
형태	동사+ing	동사+ed
의미	능동, 진행의 의미	수동, 완료의 의미
예	The news was really **shocking.**(능동) 그 소식은 정말 충격적이었다. We're **dusting** the furniture.(진행) 우리는 가구의 먼지를 털고 있다.	This house was **built** in 1990.(수동) 이 집은 1990년에 지어졌다. They've just **got** married.(완료) 그들은 방금 결혼했다.

| MORE TIPS | 현재분사와 동명사의 차이

현재분사와 동명사는 동사에 -ing를 붙인 형태이다. 둘 다 모두 동사의 성질을 갖고 있다는 점에서 동일하나, 기능적으로 현재분사는 「진행」의 의미를 가지는 '형용사' 역할을, 동명사는 「용도」나 「목적」의 의미를 가지는 '명사' 역할을 한다.

〔비교〕 (현재분사) a **sleeping** baby 잠자고 있는 아기
         (동명사) a **sleeping** pill 수면제 (취침하기 위한 약)

         (현재분사) a **smoking** man 담배 피우고 있는 남자
         (동명사) a **smoking** room 흡연실 (담배를 피우기 위한 방)

2. 분사의 동사적 역할

● 진행시제 「be동사 + 현재분사」 : ~하고 있는
    The water is **boiling.** 물이 끓고 있다.
    The population of the world is **increasing** very fast. 세계인구가 매우 빠르게 증가하고 있다.

- 수동태 「be동사 + 과거분사」 : ~하여진
  English is **used** in many countries. 영어는 많은 나라에서 사용된다.

- 완료시제 「have + 과거분사」
  I've **waited** for Susie for an hour. 나는 Susie를 한 시간 동안 기다리고 있다.

3. 분사의 형용사적 역할

- 명사 앞에서 수식 「분사 + 명사」
  분사가 단독으로 쓰였을 경우 명사 앞에서 수식한다.
  A **rolling** stone gathers no moss. 구르는 돌은 이끼가 끼지 않는다.
  Look at the **dented** car. 움푹 들어간 저 차를 봐라.

- 명사 뒤에서 수식 「명사 + 분사」
  분사가 구를 동반할 경우 명사 뒤에서 수식한다.
  The language **spoken in Canada** is English. 캐나다에서 사용되는 언어는 영어다.

- 주격보어 역할 「주어 + 동사 + 주격보어」
  현재분사는 주어와 능동적인 관계를, 과거분사는 주어와 수동적인 관계를 나타낸다.
  Sally sat **watching** TV. Sally는 TV를 보면서 앉아있었다.
  That movie was so **disappointing.** 그 영화는 매우 실망스러웠다.
  He sat **surrounded** by his fans. 그는 팬들에게 둘러싸인 채 앉아 있었다.

- 목적격보어 역할 「주어 + 동사 + 목적어 + 목적격보어」
  현재분사는 목적어와 능동적인 관계를, 과거분사는 목적어와 수동적인 관계를 나타낸다. 「주어 + 동사 + 목적어 + 현재분사/과거분사」 형태를 취할 수 있는 동사는 see, hear, feel, watch, notice, smell, find 등이다.
  I **saw** Jane **standing** at the bus stop. 나는 Jane이 버스 정류장에서 서있는 것을 봤다.
  Have you ever **heard** a canary **singing?** 너는 카나리아가 노래 부르는 것 들어봤니?
  I **found** her **running** away. 나는 그녀가 도망치는 것을 발견했다.
  I **heard** my name **called.** 나는 내 이름이 불려지는 것을 들었다.

Unit Test

1. 보기와 같은 관계가 되도록 빈칸을 채우시오.

> 보기 | interest - interesting - interested

1. excite - _____ - _____
2. write - _____ - _____
3. build - _____ - _____
4. surprise - _____ - _____
5. cut - _____ - _____

2. 둘 중 알맞은 것을 고르시오.

1. I didn't like that movie. It was (boring/ bored).
2. The woman (driving/ driven) the car was my mother.
3. I saw the tree (cutting/ cut) down.
4. Did you have your hair (cutting/ cut)?
5. You'd better keep your room (locking/ locked).
6. The police saw a man (jaywalking/ jaywalked). *jaywalk 무단횡단하다
7. Tom is one of the most (boring/ bored) people I've ever met. He never says anything (interesting/ interested).
8. I saw Jane (standing/ stood) at the bus stop.
9. The girl (smiling/ smiled) over there is my sister.
10. The car (denting/ dented) all over is my car.

3. 어법에 맞게 괄호 안의 동사를 알맞은 분사형태로 고쳐 쓰시오.

1. Look at the cat _____ (sleep) on the sofa.
2. I like _____ (mash) potatoes.
3. Listen. I have _____ (surprise) news.
4. I've worked hard all day, and now I'm _____ (exhaust).
5. I'd like to eat _____ (scramble) eggs.
6. Would you like your hair _____ (dye)?
7. The woman _____ (lean) against the wall is my aunt.
8. I came home from the meeting with _____ (mix) feelings.
9. I heard my sister _____ (weep) in her bedroom.
10. Akiko could only respond in _____ (break) English.

Writing Pattern Practice | 분사의 역할

Pattern 1_ 「be동사 + 현재분사」 진행시제

물이 끓고 있다. _____

세계 인구가 매우 빠르게 증가하고 있다.(The population of the world~)

_____

Pattern 2_ 「be동사 + 과거분사」 수동태

영어는 많은 나라에서 사용된다.(many) _____

내 차가 견인되었다.(tow away) _____

Pattern 3_ 「have + 과거분사」 완료시제

나는 Susie를 한 시간 동안 기다려왔다. _____

너를 본지도 오래 되었다.(It~, since) _____

Pattern 4_ 「분사 + 명사」 명사 앞에서 수식

구르는 돌은 이끼가 끼지 않는다.(gather, no moss) _____

움푹 들어간 저 차를 봐라.(dented car) _____

Pattern5_ 「명사 + 분사」 명사 뒤에서 수식

캐나다에서 사용되는 언어는 영어다.(spoken) _____

Pattern 6_ 「주어 + 동사 + 분사(주격보어)」 2형식 문장에서 보어역할

Sally는 TV를 보면서 앉아있었다. _____

그 영화는 매우 실망스러웠다.(That movie~, so) _____

Pattern 7_ 「주어 + 동사 + 목적어 + 분사(목적격보어)」 5형식 문장에서 보어역할

나는 Jane이 버스 정류장에서 서있는 것을 봤다. _____

너는 카나리아가 노래 부르는 것을 들어봤니?(a canary)

_____

나는 그녀가 도망치는 것을 발견했다. _____

나는 내 이름이 불려지는 것을 들었다. _____

Unit

42 분사구문

- **Pattern** 분사~, 주어 + 동사
- **Meaning** 때, 이유, 조건, 양보, 동시상황, 연속상황 등

A: Your English got much better than before.
B: Thank you.
A: When do you usually practice English?
B: While driving, I listen to English tapes all the time.

---

1. 분사구문

분사를 이용하여 부사절을 보다 간결한 부사구로 바꾼 것을 분사구문이라고 한다. 분사구문은 문장 중에서 때, 이유, 조건, 양보, 동시상황, 연속상황 등의 의미를 나타낸다.

2. 분사구문 만드는 방법

1. 접속사를 없앤다	**As I got good grades,** I was pleased. → ~~As~~ **I got good grades,** I was pleased. -①
2. 부사절의 주어와 주절의 주어가 같을 경우 부사절의 주어를 생략하고 *다를 경우 그대로 둔다	→ ~~I~~ **Got good grades,** I was pleased. -② * **As It was fine,** we went out to walk. → **It being fine,** we went out to walk.
3. 부사절의 시제와 주절의 시제가 같을 경우 「동사원형＋-ing」를 쓰고, *부사절의 시제가 주절의 시제보다 한 시제 앞설 경우 「Having＋과거분사」 형태를 쓴다	→ **Getting good grades,** I was pleased. -③ * **As I lost the money,** I can't buy the book. → **Having lost the money,** I can't buy the book.
4. 부정어(never, not)는 분사구문 앞에 위치시킨다	**As I didn't get good grades,** I was depressed. → **Not getting good grades,** I was depressed.

3. 분사구문이 현재분사로 시작하지 않는 경우

분사구문은 보통 현재분사형으로 시작하는데, 예외도 있다.

- 수동형 분사구문일 경우 – 「being+과거분사」나 「having been+과거분사」 형태에서 being 이나 having been을 생략하는 경우가 많다.
  (Being) Shocked at the news, I couldn't say a word. 그 소식에 놀라서 나는 아무 말도 할 수 없었다.
  (Having been) Ripped off by the taxi driver, he got shocked. 택시 운전사에게 사기 당하고 그는 충격을 받았다.

- 부사절의 주어와 주절의 주어가 다를 경우 – 부사절의 주어를 생략하지 않는다.
  It being cold, we didn't go out for dinner.
- 접속사의 의미를 분명하게 하고자 할 경우 – 분사 앞에 접속사를 생략하지 않을 수 있다.
  Though being very sick, I went to school.

4. 분사구문의 종류

- 때 : ~할 때
  When you take a bath, you'd better not use a hair dryer.
  → **Taking a bath,** you'd better not use a hair dryer. 목욕할 때에는 드라이어를 사용하지 않아야 한다.

- 이유 : ~이므로
  Because/ As I felt very tired, I went to bed early.
  → **Feeling very tired,** I went to bed early. 매우 피곤해서 일찍 잠자리에 들었다.

- 조건 : 만약 ~라면
  If you turn to the left, you will find the bank.
  → **Turning to the left,** you will find the bank. 왼쪽으로 돌아가시면 그 은행을 찾으실 거예요.

- 양보 : ~일지라도
  Although/ Though I understand why she did it, I still can't forgive her.
  → **Understanding why she did it,** I still can't forgive her. 그녀가 왜 그랬는지 이해는 되지만 그래도 난 그녀를 용서할 수가 없어요.

- 동시상황 : ~하면서(동시에)
  Nina checked her e-mail while she was listening to the radio.
  → Nina checked her e-mail, **listening to the radio.** Nina는 라디오를 들으면서 이메일을 확인했다.

- 연속상황 : ~하고 나서 이어
  (Right) After I got dressed, I went out with my family.
  → **Getting dressed,** I went out with my family. 옷을 입고 나서 가족들과 밖에 나갔다.

5. 분사구문의 위치

분사구문은 상황에 따라 문장의 맨 앞, 맨 뒤, 또는 문장의 중간에도 올 수 있다.
- 문장의 앞에 오는 경우
  Wearing dark glasses, the man could not see clearly. 어두운 안경을 써서 그 남자는 잘 볼 수 없었다.

- 문장의 중간에 오는 경우
  The man, **wearing dark glasses,** could not see clearly.

- 문장의 뒤에 오는 경우
  The man could not see clearly, **wearing dark glasses.**

Unit Test

1. 다음 밑줄 친 부분을 분사구문으로 바꾸시오.

1. <u>While I was walking home</u>, I saw Ted standing at the bus stop.
→ _____, I saw Ted standing at the bus stop.

2. <u>After she had finished the test</u>, she left the classroom.
→ _____, she left the classroom.

3. <u>As he was neglected by all</u>, he got angry.
→ _____, he got angry.

4. <u>If you turn to the left there</u>, you will find the building.
→ _____, you will find the building.

5. <u>As it was fine</u>, we went on a picnic.
→ _____, we went on a picnic.

6. <u>As I had seen her once before</u>, I recognized her immediately.
→ _____, I recognized her immediately.

7. <u>As I didn't receive any answer</u>, I wrote to him again.
→ _____, I wrote to him again.

8. <u>Because he is unemployed</u>, he doesn't have much money.
→ _____, he doesn't have much money.

2. 다음 밑줄 친 분사구문을 주어진 접속사를 이용하여 절로 바꾸시오.

1. <u>Returning home</u>, I found the book missing.
→ When _____, I found the book missing.

2. <u>Turning to the right</u>, you will find the station.
→ If _____, you will find the station.

3. <u>Having no money</u>, she wanted to buy that car.
→ Though _____, she wanted to buy that car.

4. <u>All things being considered</u>, he is to blame for the accident.
→ When _____, he is to blame for the accident.

5. <u>Tired out</u>, she went to bed early.
→ As _____, she went to bed early.

6. <u>Having received no answer from her</u>, I faxed her again.
→ Because _____, I faxed her again.

7. <u>Not having a car</u>, she walks to work everyday.
→ Because _____, she walks to work everyday.

Writing Pattern Practice | 분사구문

Pattern 1_ 때 : ~할 때

목욕할 때에는 드라이어를 사용하지 않아야 한다.(Taking~)

_____, you'd better not use a hair dryer.

길을 건널 때 조심해.(street)

_____, be careful.

Pattern 2_이유 : ~이므로

매우 피곤해서 일찍 잠자리에 들었다.(Feeling~)

_____, I went to bed early.

돈이 없어서 그 집을 살 수 없다.

_____, I can't buy that house.

Pattern 3_조건 : 만약 ~라면

왼쪽으로 돌아가시면 그 은행을 찾으실 거예요.

_____, you will find the bank.

Pattern 4_양보 : ~일지라도

네가 하는 말을 이해는 하지만 나는 여전히 그것을 안 믿는다.(what you say)

_____, I still don't believe it.

Pattern 5_동시상황 : ~하면서 (동시에)

Nina는 라디오를 들으면서 이메일을 확인했다.

Nina checked her e-mail,_____

Pattern 6_연속상황 : ~하고 나서 이어

옷을 입고 나서 가족들과 밖에 나갔다.(get dressed)

_____, I went out with my family.

Pattern 7_분사구문의 부정

무엇을 해야 할지 몰라서 나는 그녀의 조언을 구했다.(what to do)

_____, I asked for her advice.

43 분사구문의 의미상주어/ 부대상황

● **Pattern** 독립분사구문

with + 명사 + 분사/ 형용사/ 부사(구)

Grammar in Practice

A: I wish you wouldn't watch TV.

B: Sorry. Were you trying to sleep?

A: Yes, I can hardly sleep with the TV on. I have an important meeting tomorrow morning.

B: OK. I'll turn it off.

Grammar in Use

1. 비인칭 독립분사 구문

분사구문의 의미상 주어가 we, you, they 등 일반인이 주어인 경우, 의미상 주어를 생략하고 쓰는 것이 보통이다. 이를 보통 「비인칭 독립분사구문」이라 한다.

2. 자주 사용하는 비인칭 독립분사 구문

considering (that) ~을 감안한다면	judging from ~로 판단하건대
speaking of ~에 관해 말하자면	admitting that ~은 인정하지만
strictly speaking 엄밀히 말하자면	granted that ~은 인정하지만
compared with ~을 비교하면	frankly speaking 솔직히 말하자면
seeing that ~을 보면, ~이므로	provided that = providing that ~라면

Considering his age, he's in good shape. 그의 나이를 고려하면 그는 몸매가 좋다.

Judging from his accent, he seems to be an American. 그의 억양으로 판단하건대 그는 미국인인 것 같다.

Speaking of bears, here is a story for you. 곰에 대해 말하자면 당신에게 해 줄 이야기가 있다.

Strictly speaking, she is not so good at math. 엄격히 말하면 그녀는 수학을 그렇게 잘하는 것이 아니다.

Granted that you were drunk, you should be responsible for your conduct. 술 취했다는 것을 인정한다 하더라도 당신은 당신 행동에 책임을 져야 한다.

Compared with last year, the birthrate in Korea has decreased. 작년과 비교해 한국의 출생률은 감소했다.

Frankly speaking, I didn't do my homework yet. 솔직히 말해 난 아직 숙제를 하지 않았다.

His English is not bad, **seeing that** he has learned it for six months. 영어를 배운지 겨우 6개월이라는 점에서 보면 그의 영어실력은 나쁘지 않다.

Provided that all your work is done, you may go home. 일이 다 끝나면 당신은
집에 가도 좋다.
= **Providing** that all your work is done, you may go home.

3. **with를 이용한 부대상황 「with + 명사 + 보어」**

「with + 명사 + 보어」 구문은 '명사가 ～(보어)한 채로' 라는 뜻으로 한꺼번에 두 가지 일을 말할
때 사용한다. 이때 보어가 분사일 경우, 명사와의 관계가 능동이면 현재분사, 수동이면 과거분사
를 사용한다.

● 「with + 명사 + V-ing」
  It was a misty morning, **with little wind blowing.** 바람이 거의 불지 않는 안개 낀 아
  침이었다.

● 「with + 명사 + V-ed」
  She is singing, **with her eyes closed.** 그녀는 눈을 감은 채로 노래를 부르고 있다.
  With an eye bandaged, I could not read properly. 눈에 붕대를 감은 채 나는 제대로
  읽을 수 없었다.

● 「with + 명사 + 형용사/부사(구)」
  Don't speak **with your mouth full.** 음식물을 입에 가득 넣은 채로 이야기하지 마라.
  He was standing, **with his hands in his pockets.** 그는 손을 주머니에 넣은 채로 서
  있었다.

| MORE TIPS | 자주 사용하는 with를 이용한 부대상황 표현

1. 「with + 명사 + V-ing」
• with one's hair waving in the wind 머리카락을 바람에 날리면서
• with one's dog following behind 개가 뒤에서 따르고
• with one's jacket hanging on one's shoulder 상의를 어깨에 걸치고 *hang 매달리다, 걸리다

2. 「with + 명사 + V-ed」
• with one's legs crossed(folded) 다리를 꼬고
• with one's arms crossed 팔짱을 끼고
• with one's eye bandaged 한쪽 눈을 붕대로 감고

3. 「with + 명사 + 형용사/부사(구)」
• with a radio on/off 라디오를 켜놓은 채/꺼놓은 채
• with one's mouth full 입안을 가득 채우고
• with a smile on one's face 얼굴에 미소를 띠며
• with a pipe in one's mouth 파이프를 입에 물고
• with a hat on/off 모자를 쓴 채로/벗은 채로
• with one's hand in one's pocket 손을 주머니에 찔러 넣은 채로

Unit Test

1. 보기에서 문맥상 가장 알맞은 독립분사구문을 골라 빈칸에 써 넣으시오.

> 보기 | judging from   granted that   compared with   frankly speaking   speaking of

1. _____ traveling, Jeju island is the best place in Korea.
2. _____, this book is not as interesting as I thought.
3. Male unemployment was 34.2%, _____ 45.8% for women.
4. _____ his accent, he's a German.
5. _____ he doesn't look too bad for his age, I don't fancy him.

2. 괄호안의 단어를 알맞은 형태의 분사로 바꿔 쓰시오.

1. He fell asleep with the TV _____ (turn) on.
2. Laura came in the room with her puppy _____ (follow) her.
3. My father came into the living room with his eye _____ (bandage).
4. She is singing, with her eyes _____ (close).
5. I was sitting with my legs _____ (cross).

3. 우리말과 일치하도록 괄호 안의 단어를 알맞게 배열하시오.

1. 그녀는 불을 켜 놓은 채 잠이 들었다. (fell asleep/ with/ she/ the lights/ on)

_____

2. 음식물을 입에 가득 넣은 채로 이야기하지 마라. (with/ don't speak/ full/ your mouth)

_____

3. 그녀는 얼굴에 미소를 띠며 방에 들어왔다. (came into the room/ she/ on her face/ with a smile)

_____

4. 그는 입을 벌린 채로 자고 있다. (is sleeping/ with/ open/ he/ his mouth)

_____

5. 그는 라디오를 켜 놓은 채 공부하고 있다. (with/ turned on/ he's studying/ the radio)

_____

Writing Pattern Practice | 분사구문의 의미상 주어/ 부대상황

그의 나이를 고려하면 그는 테니스를 잘 친다.

_____, he plays tennis well.

그의 억양으로 판단하건대 그는 미국인인 것 같다.

_____, he seems to be an American.

당신이 술 취했다는 것을 인정한다 하더라도 당신 행동에 책임을 져야 한다.

_____, you are responsible for your conduct.

솔직히 말해 그녀의 영어는 별로다.

_____, her English is not so good.

엄격히 말하면 그녀는 수학을 그렇게 잘하는 것이 아니다.

_____, she is not so good at math.

일이 다 끝나면 당신은 집에 가도 좋다.

_____ all your work is done, you may go home.

영어를 배운지 겨우 6개월이라는 점에서 보면 그의 영어실력은 나쁘지 않다.

His English is not bad, _____ he has learned it for six months.

● 「with + 명사 + V-ing」
그녀는 머리카락을 바람에 날리면서 길을 따라 걸었다.(walk along)

_____

● 「with +명사 + V-ed」
그녀는 눈을 감은 채로 노래를 부르고 있다.   _____
입 다문 채로 그것을 들어.(listen, shut)   _____

● 「with + 명사 + 형용사/부사(구)」
음식물을 입에 가득 넣은 채로 이야기하지 마라.   _____
그는 손을 주머니에 넣은 채로 서 있었다.(He was standing, ~)

_____

그녀는 모자를 쓴 채로 방에 들어갔다.(go into, on)_____

Unit

44 수동태

● **Pattern**   주어 + be동사 + pp(과거분사)
● **Meaning**   ~되다, ~당하다

Grammar in Practice

(At the shopping mall)

A: Are you being helped?

B: No. I'd like a long-sleeved shirt in white, medium.

A: Here's a good one. This is 30% off.

B: Great.

Grammar in Use

1. 수동태

능동태는 행위의 주체가 주어로 표현된 형식이고 수동태는 행위의 대상이 주어로 표현된 형식이다.

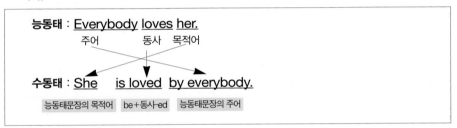

능동태 : Everybody loves her.
      주어   동사   목적어

수동태 : She   is loved by everybody.
      능동태문장의 목적어   be+동사-ed   능동태문장의 주어

| MORE TIPS | 수동태에서 「be+동사-ed」 대신 「get+-동사-ed」를 쓰기도 한다.
John **got arrested** for drunken driving yesterday. John은 어제 음주운전으로 체포되었다.

2. 수동태의 주요시제

수동태시제	구조	예
현재시제	am/are/is+pp	English **is spoken** in Canada.
현재진행시제	am/are/is+being+pp	Look! Your car **is being towed.**
과거시제	was/were+pp	**Were** you **invited** to the party?
과거진행시제	was/were+being+pp	The house **was being painted.**
현재완료시제	have/has+been pp	I **have been promoted.**
과거완료시제	had+been+pp	The singer knew he **had been forgotten.**
미래시제(will)	will be+pp	You**'ll be told** soon.
미래완료시제(will)	will have been+pp	This report **will have been done** by tomorrow.
미래시제(be going to)	am/are/is going to be+pp	Who**'s going to** be fired?

3. 수동태를 쓰는 경우

행위에 영향을 받는 대상, 즉 목적어에 관심이 있는 경우 수동태를 쓴다.

Paper **was invented** by the Chinese. 종이는 중국사람들에 의해 만들어졌다.

Sally **is being interviewed** now. Sally는 지금 인터뷰를 받고 있다.

이때 관심대상이 아닌 「by+행위자」는 생략되는 경우도 많다.

*「by+행위자」를 생략하는 경우

● 행위자가 누구인지 중요하지 않거나 모르는 경우

This building **was built** in 1960. 이 빌딩은 1960년에 지어졌다.

My car **was stolen** yesterday. 내 차가 어제밤 도난당했다.

● 행위자가 막연한 일반인일 경우

Chinese **is spoken** in Singapore. 중국어는 싱가폴에서 쓰인다.

4. 수동태를 쓰지 않는 경우

● 목적어를 취하지 않는 자동사는 수동태를 사용할 수 없다.

I slept. → I was slept. (X)

| MORE TIPS | 자동사라해도 전치사와 결합해 대상이 되는 명사가 생기면 수동태를 만들 수도 있다.

〈능〉 Cindy is looking after her son.
〈수〉 Her son **is being looked after** by Cindy.

〈능〉 Someone broke into my house last night.
〈수〉 My house **was broken into** last night.

● 수동태가 불가능한 타동사들도 있다. 주로 소유관계나 상태를 나타내는 동사들이다.

have ~을 가지다 own ~을 소유하다 suit ~에 어울리다 resemble ~을 닮다 등

He **has** a sense of humor. (O) 그는 유머감각이 있다.

→A sense of humor is had by him. (X)

This coat **suits** you very well. (O) 이 코트는 너에게 매우 잘 어울린다.

→You are suited very well by this coat. (X)

Unit Test

1. 다음 문장을 수동태 문장으로 바꾸시오.

1. Shakespeare wrote *Hamlet.*

→ _____

2. A friend of mine is repairing the roof.

→ _____

3. People in Chile speak Spanish.

→ _____

4. They built this house in 1980.

→ _____

5. This book will change your life.

→ _____

6. The police have arrested Adam.

→ _____

7. The secretary was preparing the papers then.

→ _____

8. Electricity drives this car.

→ _____

9. Dangerous driving causes many accidents.

→ _____

10. The company is going to employ three hundred people.

→ _____

2. 괄호 안의 동사를 이용하여 빈칸에 채워 수동태 문장을 완성하시오. 주어진 시제를 참고하시오.

1. He is _____ (call) Mr. Perfect. 현재시제
2. Those pyramids _____ (build) around 400 AD. 과거시제
3. The results _____ (analyze). 현재완료시제
4. I found that all money _____ (steal). 과거완료시제
5. The house _____ (paint). 현재진행시제
6. I felt I _____ (follow). 과거진행시제
7. You will _____ (tell) soon. 미래시제
8. The meeting will _____ (do) by noon. 미래완료시제

Writing Pattern Practice | 수동태

Pattern 1_ 수동태 현재시제 「am/are/is + pp」

캐나다에서는 영어가 쓰인다.(speak) _____

이 방은 매일 청소되어진다. _____

Pattern 2_ 수동태 현재진행시제 「am/are/is + being + pp」

네 차가 견인되고 있다.(tow) _____

Alex가 벌받고 있다.(punish) _____

Pattern 3_ 수동태 과거시제 「was/were + pp」

너는 그 파티에 초대되었니? _____

이 식탁은 할아버지에 의해 만들어졌다. _____

Pattern 4_ 수동태 과거진행시제 「was/were + being + pp」

그 집이 페인트칠해지고 있었다. _____

Pattern 5_ 수동태 현재완료시제 「have/has + been + pp」

나는 진급되었다.(promote) _____

Adam이 체포되었다.(arrest) _____

Pattern 6_ 수동태 과거완료시제 「had + been + pp」

그 가수는 그가 잊혀졌다는 것을 알았다. _____

Pattern 7_ 수동태 미래시제(will) 「will be + pp」

너는 곧 듣게 될거야.(tell) _____

Pattern 8_ 수동태 미래완료시제(will) 「will have been + pp」

이 보고서는 내일까지 끝나게 될 거야.(do) _____

Pattern 9_ 수동태 미래시제(be going to) 「am/are/is going to be + pp」

누가 해고 당할까?(Who's~, fire) _____

누가 초대 받을까? _____

45_ 그 밖의 여러가지 수동태

● Pattern   주어 + be동사 + pp(과거분사)
● Meaning ～되다, ～당하다

Grammar in Practice

A: May I be excused for a moment?
B: Sure.
A: I'll be back in a couple of minutes.
B: OK. Take your time.

Grammar in Use

1. 명령문의 수동태

명령문은 주어를 쓰지 않는 것이 원칙이므로 수동태에서도 「by+행위자」를 쓰지 않는다.

● 긍정명령문 「Let + 목적어 + be + pp」
〈능〉 Do it. → 〈수〉 Let it **be done.** 그것을 하게끔 해라.

● 부정명령문 「Let + 목적어 + not + be + pp」 또는 「Don't + let + 목적어 + be + pp」
〈능〉 Don't do it. → 〈수〉 Let it **not be done.** (=**Don't** let it **be done.**) 그것을 행
해지지 않게 해라.

2. 조동사가 있는 수동태

조동사 뒤에 be동사의 원형인 be를 쓴다. 「조동사+be+pp」
This report **must be finished** by tomorrow. 이보고서는 내일까지 끝마쳐져야 한다.
May I be excused for a moment? 제가 잠시 실례해도 될까요?

3. to부정사의 수동태

to부정사 뒤에 be동사의 원형인 be를 쓴다. 「to부정사+be+pp」
I'm glad **to be invited** to the party. 나는 파티에 초대 되어서 기쁘다.
Most people like **to be given** presents. 대부분 사람들은 선물 받는 것을 좋아한다.

4. 동명사의 수동태

be동사의 동명사 형태인 being을 쓴다. 「being+pp」
I hate **being treated** unfairly. 나는 불공평하게 취급받는 것이 싫어.
I don't like **being told** what to do. 나는 무엇을 할지 말 듣는 것을 좋아하지 않는다.
Nobody likes **being kept** waiting. 아무도 계속 기다리게 되는 것을 좋아하지 않는다.

5. by 대신 사용되는 전치사

능동태 문장을 수동태 문장으로 전환 할때 능동태 문장의 주어는 수동태 문장에서 주로 전치사 by 뒤에 위치시킨다. 하지만 이때 내용상이나 관용적으로 by 이외에 다른 전치사를 쓰기도 한다.

● 전치사 to를 쓰는 경우: '～에게', '～에'

be known to ～에게 알려지다 **be sent to** ～에게 보내지다 **be engaged to** ～와 약혼하다 **be accustomed to** ～에 익숙해지다

Eric **is known to** everybody in this town. Eric은 이 마을의 모든 사람들에게 알려져 있다.
I'm not accustomed to making a speech in public. 나는 사람들 앞에서 이야기하는 것에 익숙하지 않다.

| MORE TIPS | be known 다음에 항상 to가 오는 것이 아니라 상황에 따라 be known by(～에 의하여 알 수 있다), be known for(～로 유명하다), be known as (～로 알려져 있다) 등처럼 다양한 전치사가 올 수 있다.

● 전치사 with를 쓰는 경우: '～로', ' ～(상황)과 함께'

be satisfied with ～에 만족하다   **be pleased with** ～에 기뻐하다
be covered with ～으로 가득 차 있다   **be impressed with** ～에 감명받다

I'm satisfied with my new job. 나는 내 새로운 일에 만족한다.
I was impressed with his speech. 나는 그의 연설에 감명받았다.

● 전치사 at을 쓰는 경우: '(어떤 정보)에'

be surprised at ～에 놀라다   **be shocked at** ～에 충격받다
be disappointed at ～에 실망하다

I was surprised at the news. 나는 그 소식에 놀랐다.

● 전치사 about을 쓰는 경우: '(어떤 상황)에 대해'

be concerned about ～에 대해 걱정한다 **be worried about** ～에 대해 걱정한다

I'm worried about your health. 나는 네 건강을 걱정하고 있어.
We're concerned about rising gas prices. 우리는 휘발유 가격 상승에 대해 염려하고 있다.

Unit Test

1. 보기의 동사를 이용하여 수동태 문장을 완성하시오.

보기 | love   pay   do   wake up

1. 그것을 하게끔 해라.

   Let it _____.

2. 당신은 그 일을 하는데 500달러를 지불받을 거에요.

   You will _____ $500 to do the work.

3. 모든 사람들은 사랑 받는 것을 좋아한다.

   Everybody likes to _____.

4. 우리는 시끄러운 소리에 잠이 깨여졌다.

   We were _____ by a loud noise.

2. 빈칸에 들어갈 알맞은 전치사를 보기에서 골라 써 넣으시오.(중복가능)

보기 | to   with   at   about

1. 편지가 Jim에게 보내졌다.

   A letter was sent _____ Jim.

2. 나는 Tim과 약혼했다.

   I'm engaged _____ Tim.

3. 나는 그들의 공연에 감명 받았다.

   I was impressed _____ their performance.

4. 그녀는 나의 사업에 대하여 걱정했다.

   She was concerned _____ my business.

5. 나는 그 소식에 놀랐다.

   I was shocked _____ the news.

6. 너는 새로운 직업에 만족하니?

   Are you satisfied _____ your new job?

7. 내 눈은 어둠에 익숙해 졌다.

   My eyes got accustomed _____ the dark.

3. 우리말과 일치하도록 괄호 안의 단어를 알맞게 배열하시오.

1. Elvis Presley는 1935년에 태어났다. (was born/ Elvis Presley/ in 1935)

   _____

2. 캐나다에서는 영어가 쓰인다. (in Canada/ is/ English / spoken)

   _____

3. 이 빌딩은 100년 전에 세워졌니? (this building/ was/ 100 years ago/ built/ ?)

   _____

Writing Pattern Practice | 그 밖의 여러가지 수동태

Pattern 1_ 「Let + 목적어 + be + pp」, 「Let + 목적어 + not + be + pp」 또는 「Don't + let + 목적어 + be + pp」 명령문수동태

그것을 하게끔 해라.(do)　　　　　_____

이 칼이 만져지지 않게 해라.(touch)　_____

(=Don't let this knife be touched.)

Pattern 2_ 「조동사 + be + pp」 조동사가 있는 수동태

이 보고서는 내일까지 끝마쳐져야 한다.(must)　_____

너는 100달러를 받을 거야.(will, give)　　　　_____

Pattern 3_ 「to부정사 + be + pp」 to부정사의 수동태

나는 파티에 초대되어서 기쁘다.(glad)　　　　_____

대부분 사람들은 선물 받는 것을 좋아한다.(presents)　_____

Pattern 4_ 「being + pp」 동명사의 수동태

나는 불공평하게 취급받는 것이 싫어.(unfairly)　_____

나는 무엇을 할지 말 듣는 것을 좋아하지 않는다.(tell, what to do)　_____

아무도 계속 기다리게 되는 것을 좋아하지 않는다.(Nobody, keep waiting)　_____

Pattern 5_ 「to, with, at, about + 행위자」 by 대신 사용되는 전치사

Eric은 이 마을의 모든 사람들에게 알려져 있다.(everybody, in this town)

_____

나는 내 새로운 일에 만족한다.　　　_____

나는 그 소식에 놀랐다.(surprise)　　_____

나는 너에 대해 염려하고 있어.(concern)　_____

Unit
46_ 주의해야할 수동태

- **Pattern**   주어 + be동사 + pp(과거분사)
- **Meaning** ~되다, ~당하다

A: What a nice sweater!
B: Yes, it is! It was made for me by my grandma.
A: Really? She's *handy with a needle. That looks good on you.
B: Thanks.

*handy 솜씨 좋은

1. 동사구 수동태

두개 이상의 단어가 모여서 동사 역할을 하는 것을 동사구(「동사＋부사/전치사」, 「동사＋명사/부사＋전치사」)라고 한다.

이때 동사구는 하나의 동사처럼 취급하여 수동태를 만든다.

〈능〉「주어＋ 동사구＋목적어」
→ 〈수〉「주어(능동태 문장의 목적어)＋be동사＋동사구(pp형태) (＋by＋행위자)」

〈능〉 Everybody laughed at me. 모두가 나를 비웃었다.
〈수〉 I **was laughed at by** Everybody. 나는 모두에게 비웃음을 당했다.

〈능〉 I always make a fool of Sally's big nose. 나는 항상 Sally의 큰 코를 놀린다.
〈수〉 Sally's big nose **is** always **made a fool of by** me. Sally의 큰 코는 항상 나에게 놀림을 당한다.

2. 4형식 문장(목적어가 두개인 문장) 수동태

「주어＋동사＋간접목적어＋직접목적어」 형태의 4형식 문장을 수동태로 만드는 경우에서는 어느 것이 강조되는 상황이냐에 따라 간접목적어와 직접목적어 모두를 주어로 취할 수 있다.

〈능〉「주어＋동사(대부분의 4형식동사)＋간접목적어＋직접목적어」
→ 〈수1〉「주어(간접목적어)＋be동사＋pp＋직접목적어 (＋by＋행위자)」
→ 〈수2〉「주어(직접목적어)＋be동사＋pp＋전치사(to/for~)＋간접목적어 (＋by＋행위자)」

〈능〉 Kevin gave me a present. Kevin은 나에게 선물을 줬다.
〈수1〉 I **was given** a present by Kevin. 나는 Kevin에게 선물을 받았다.
〈수2〉 A present **was given to** me by Kevin. 선물은 Kevin에 의해 주어졌다.

| MORE TIPS | 4형식 동사 중 make나 buy의 경우 간접목적어 앞에 to 대신 for를 쓰고 또한 직접목적어만 수동태 문장의 주어가 될 수 있음을 유의한다. 직접목적어만 수동태 문장의 주어가 될 수 있는 4형식 동사는 make, buy, send, pass, write 등이 있다.

〈능〉 My mother made me this sweater. 엄마가 이 스웨터를 내게 만들어주셨다.
〈수1〉 This sweater **was made for** me by my mother. 이 스웨터는 나를 위해 엄마에 의해 만들어졌다.
〈수2〉 I was made this sweater by my mother. (X)

3. 5형식 문장(목적어와 목적보어가 있는 문장) 수동태

「주어 + 동사 + 목적어 + 목적보어」 형태의 5형식 문장을 수동태로 만들기 위해서는 일반적으로 목적어를 수동태문장의 주어로 쓰고 목적격 보어를 그대로 쓴다. 하지만 상황에 따라 보어가 to 부정사 등으로 바뀌는 경우도 있다.

〈능〉「주어 + 목적어 + 목적격보어」

→ 〈수〉「주어(능동태 문장의 목적어) + be동사 + pp + 목적격보어 (+ by + 행위자)」

〈능〉Everybody calls him a fool. 모든 사람이 그를 바보라고 부른다.

〈수〉He **is called** a fool (by everybody). 그는 (모든 사람에 의해) 바보라고 불린다.

〈능〉I thought him a great singer. 나는 그를 훌륭한 가수라고 생각한다.

〈수〉He **was thought** a great singer. 그는 훌륭한 가수라고 생각되어졌다.

〈능〉My boss made me work overtime. 상사는 나를 초과근무 시켰다.

〈수〉I **was made to** work overtime by my boss. 나는 상사에 의해 초과근무 시켜졌다.

| MORE TIPS | 사역동사 make를 이용한 「make + 목적어 + 동사원형」 문장을 수동태 문장으로 만들 경우 목적보어인 '동사 원형'은 'to부정사' 형태가 된다는 점을 유의한다.

4. 목적어가 명사절일 때 수동태

목적어가 명사절일 경우 수동태 문장에서 가주어 it을 사용한다. It is thought that ~, It is believed that ~, It is expected that ~ 등이 이와 같은 구조이다. 또한 명사절의 주어를 문장의 주어로 쓰는 경우에는 that 절의 동사는 to부정사로 바꿔 쓴다.

〈능〉「주어 + 동사 + 목적어(명사절)」

→ 〈수1〉「It(가주어) + is/was + pp + that + 주어 + 동사」
　　　「주어(능동태 문장의 목적어) + be동사 + pp (+ by + 행위자)」

→ 〈수2〉「주어(명사절의 주어) + be동사 + pp + to + 동사원형」

〈능〉They say that he is honest. 사람들은 그가 정직하다고 말한다.

〈수〉That he is honest is said (by them) 그는 정직하다는 말은 듣는다.

　　→ **It is said that** he is honest. 가주어 It 사용

　　→ **He is said to** be honest. 명사절의 주어를 문장의 주어로 쓰는 경우

〈능〉They expect that the strike will end soon. 그들은 파업이 곧 중단될 것이라고 예상한다.

〈수〉That the strike will end soon is expected by them. 파업이 곧 중단될 것이라고 그들에 의해 예상된다.

　　→ **It is expected that** the strike will end soon. 가주어 It 사용

　　→ **The strike is expected to** end soon. 명사절의 주어를 문장의 주어로 쓰는 경우

Unit Test

1. 다음 문장을 수동태 문장으로 바꾸시오.

1. Mary takes care of my baby.
→ _____

2. David laughed at me.
→ _____

3. Everybody looks up to Professor Lee.
→ _____

4. Kevin gave me a present.
→ I _____
→ A present _____

5. They gave the winner a prize.
→ The winner _____
→ A prize _____

6. Someone made Kate this cake.
→ This cake _____

7. They call him a fool.
→ _____

8. The doctor made him stop smoking.
→ _____

9. They say that he is a nice person.
→ It _____
→ He _____

10. They believed that the Earth was flat.
→ It _____
→ The Earth _____

2. 우리말과 일치하도록 괄호 안의 단어를 알맞게 배열하시오.

1. 그는 천재로 간주 되었다. (was/ he/ a genius/ considered)
→ _____

2. 그는 바보로 불린다. (is/ he/ stupid/ called)
→ _____

3. 아무 것도 내게 보내지지 않았다. (was/ to me/ nothing/ sent)
→ _____

4. 이야기들이 아이들에게 읽혀졌다. (were/ stories/ to the children/ read)
→ _____

36

Writing Pattern Practice | 주의해야할 수동태

Pattern 1_ 「주어(능동태 문장의 목적어) + be동사 + 동사구(pp형태) (+ by + 행위자)」 동사구 수동태

나는 모두에게 비웃음을 당했다.(laugh at) _____

Sally의 큰 코는 항상 나에게 놀림을 당한다.(make a fool of) _____

_____

내 아기는 Mary에 의해서 돌보아진다.(take care of) _____

Pattern 2_ 「주어(간접목적어) + be동사 + pp + 직접목적어 (+ by + 행위자)」 4형식 문장(목적어가 두개인 문장) 수동태
「주어(직접목적어) + be동사 + pp + 전치사(to/for~) + 간접목적어 (+ by + 행위자)」

나는 Kevin에게 선물을 받았다.(be given) _____

이 스웨터는 나를 위해 만들어졌다. _____

상이 우승자에게 주어졌다.(A prize, be given) _____

프랑스어가 Mrs. Lee에 의해 우리에게 가르쳐진다. _____

Pattern 3_ 「주어(능동태 문장의 목적어) + be동사 + pp + 목적격보어 (+ by + 행위자)」 5형식 문장(목적어와 목적보어가 있는 문장) 수동태

그는 바보로 불려진다.(a fool) _____

그는 훌륭한 가수로 간주되었다.(be thought) _____

나는 나의 상사에 의해 초과근무를 하도록 만들어 졌다.(work overtime) _____

_____

나는 매우 행복하게 만들어졌다.(I have been~) _____

Pattern 4_ 「It(가주어) + is/was + pp + that + 주어 + 동사」 목적어가 명사절인 문장 수동태
「주어(능동태 문장의 목적어) + be동사 + pp (+ by + 행위자)」
「주어(명사절의 주어) + be동사 + pp + to + 동사원형」

그는 정직하다고 말 되어진다.(It is said that~) _____

(He is said~) _____

그 파업이 곧 끝날 거라고 예상된다.(end) _____

(It is expected that~) _____

(The strike is expected~) _____

Unit

47 to부정사

● **Pattern** to + 동사원형 : 명사, 형용사, 부사역할

A: Oh, I want to eat that pizza.
B: Let's go in and have some!
A: No. I'm on a diet. I don't want to break my *New Year's resolution.
B: I think you should lose weight by exercising regularly.

*New Year's resolution 새해 다짐, 결의

1. to부정사 「to + 동사원형」의 쓰임

쓰임	문장에서 역할	예문
명사 역할	주어역할	**To exercise** everyday isn't easy. = It isn't easy **to exercise** everyday.
	목적어역할	I love **to meet** people. I thought it easy **to get** a high TOEIC score. (가목적어)
	보어역할	My plan is **to fly** to New York this weekend.
형용사 역할	명사, 대명사 수식	E-mail is the easiest way **to contact** Kate. You have the right **to remain** silent. Get me a chair **to sit on**. I will get you something **to drink**.
	보어 : 주격보어(예정,의무, 조건,가능,운명 등) 목적격보어	Sarah **is** soon **to be** his wife. (예정) I set my goal **to be rich**.
부사 역할	동사, 형용사, 부사, 문장전체 수식 (목적, 결과, 원인, 조건, 양보, 판단의 근거, 정도 등)	I came here **to help** you. (동사수식) This coffee is hot **to drink**. (형용사수식) You're old enough **to support** yourself. (부사수식) **To tell the truth,** she is a stalker. (문장전체수식) *문장 전체를 수식하는 to부정사 구문은 다음과 같은 것들이 있다. • to make matters worse 설상가상으로, • strange to say 이상한 얘기지만, • not to mention ~는 말할 것도 없이, • to begin with 우선 • needless to say 말할 필요도 없이

2. to부정사의 시제

● 단순시제 : 「to + 동사원형」

본동사의 시제와 같으나 나중(미래)시제를 의미한다.

I want **to see** the manager. 나는 매니저를 만나고 싶어.

● 진행시제 : 「to + be + 동사-ing」

진행시제는 본동사와 같은 시점에 진행 중인 동작을 의미한다.

He seems **to be studying** in his room. 그는 방에서 공부 중인 것 같다.

● 완료시제 : 「to + have + pp」

완료시제는 본동사보다 과거의 사실을 의미한다.

I'm sorry **to have kept** you waiting. 기다리게 해서 미안합니다.

3. to부정사의 부정

to부정사 앞에 not, never 등의 부정어를 쓴다.

I tried **not to bother** my father. 나는 아버지를 귀찮게 해드리지 않기 위해 노력했다.

I'm sorry **not to have** called you. 너에게 전화 못해서 미안해.

4. 행위자를 나타내는 표현

to부정사는 동사의 변형된 형태로 동사처럼 to부정사 또한 그 동작의 주체가 있게 된다. 이를 부정사의 의미상의 주어라고 하는데 문장의 주어와 일치하거나 일반인일 경우 밝히지 않기도 한다.

1. 의미상 주어를 밝히는 경우

● 보통 「for + 목적격」형태로 to부정사 앞에 쓴다.

It's difficult **for me to get** up early. 내가 일찍 일어나는 것은 어렵다.

It's unusual **for him to joke.** 그가 농담을 하는 것은 이례적인 일이다.

● 다음과 같이 사람의 성질을 나타내는 형용사가 사용된 경우 「of + 목적격」 형태로 쓴다.

brave	bad	careful	careless	clever
stupid	foolish	polite	nice	kind
cruel(잔인한)	sweet(다정한)	generous(관대한)	considerate(사려깊은)	

It was **careless of you to say** that. 그런 말을 하다니 부주의했어.

It was **sweet of you to remember** my birthday. 내 생일을 기억하다니 다정했어.

2. 의미상 주어를 밝히지 않는 경우

● 의미상의 주어가 문장의 주어와 일치하는 경우

I want **to be** a singer. (의미상의 주어 : I) 나는 가수가 되고 싶다.

● 의미상의 주어가 문장의 목적어와 일치하는 경우

I want you **to be** a singer. (의미상의 주어 : you) 나는 네가 가수가 되었으면 좋겠다.

● 의미상의 주어가 일반인 주어일 경우

It's important **to exercise** regularly. (의미상의 주어 : everybody) 정기적으로 운동하는 것은 중요하다.

Unit Test

1. 보기와 같이 밑줄친 to부정사의 쓰임을 빈칸에 써 넣으시오.

> 보기 | decided <u>to take</u> a taxi home. (명사)

1. I promised not <u>to be</u> late. (   )
2. This coffee is hot <u>to drink</u>. (   )
3. Do you like <u>to meet</u> people? (   )
4. It's nice <u>to hear</u> from you. (   )
5. <u>To tell the truth</u>, she's not my girlfriend. (   )
6. Give me something <u>to write on</u>. (   )
7. It's important <u>to exercise</u>. (   )

2. 둘 중 알맞은 것을 고르시오.

1. This house is big enough (for/ of) your family to live in.
2. It was careless (for/ of) you to say so.
3. It was kind (for/ of) Ann to give me a ride.
4. This vacuum cleaner might be convenient (for/ of) you to use.
5. It was foolish (for/ of) you to do that.

3. 우리말과 일치하도록 괄호 안의 단어를 알맞게 배열하시오.

1. 네 필체는 읽기 불가능하다. (to read/ is impossible/ your handwriting)

_____

2. 나는 그녀를 본 것이 기쁘다. (to/ I'm glad/ have seen her)

_____

3. 내가 Ted를 짜증나게 한 것 같다. (to/ I seem/ have annoyed Ted)

_____

4. 너와 저녁을 함께 하고 있어서 좋아. (having dinner with you/ nice/ it's/ to be)

_____

5. 늦지 않도록 노력해. (to be late/ not/ try)

_____

6. 사람들 말을 듣는 것은 중요하다. (important/ to /it's/ listen to people)

_____

7. 나는 중고차는 사지 않기로 결정했다. (I/ not to/ decided/ a used car/ buy)

_____

Writing Pattern Practice | to부정사

Pattern 1_ to부정사 : 명사역할

매일 운동하는 것은 쉽지 않다.(It~) _____

나는 사람들 만나는 것을 좋아한다.(love) _____

Pattern 2_ to부정사 : 형용사역할

앉을 의자를 내게 가져다줘.(get) _____

내가 너에게 마실 것 좀 가져다 줄게. _____

Pattern 3_ to부정사 : 부사역할

그녀는 버스를 잡기위해 뛰었다. _____

이 커피는 마시기에 너무 뜨거워. _____

사실상 그녀는 스토커다.(a stalker) _____

Pattern 4_ 「to + 동사원형」 to부정사의 단순시제

나는 너와 말하고 싶어.(want, talk) _____

Pattern 5_ 「to + be + 동사-ing」 to부정사의 진행시제

그는 방에서 공부 중인 것 같다.(seem) _____

Pattern 6_ 「to + have + pp」 to부정사의 완료시제

당신을 계속 기다리게 해서 미안합니다. _____

내가 어제 Mary를 짜증나게 한 것 같다.(I seem to~, annoy) _____

Pattern 7_ 「not to + 동사원형」 to부정사의 부정

나는 아버지를 귀찮게 해드리지 않기 위해 노력했다. _____

Pattern 8_ 「for/ of + 목적격 + to + 동사원형」 to부정사의 의미상 주어

모두가 잠자리에 들 시간이다.(It's time~) _____

그가 농담을 하는 것은 흔치 않은 일이다.(unusual) _____

그런 말을 하다니 너는 부주의했어.(careless) _____

내 생일을 기억하다니 너는 다정했어.(sweet) _____

_____

48 동사 + to부정사, 동사 + 목적어 +to부정사, 의문사 + to부정사

● **Pattern** 동사+to부정사
동사+목적어+to부정사
의문사+to부정사

A: Excuse me. Could you tell me how to get to Main street?

B: Keep going straight for three blocks. It's right there.

A: Is it too far to walk?

B: No, It's only a five-minute walk.

---

1. 「동사 + to부정사」

다음은 to부정사를 목적어로 가지는 동사들이다.

agree	ask	decide	expect	fail	hope
offer	promise	refuse	want	wish	plan

I **want to go** alone. 나는 혼자 가기를 원한다.
We **expected to be** late. 우리는 늦을 거라고 예상했다.

2. 「동사 + 목적어 + to부정사」

다음은 to부정사 앞에 목적어를 써서 「동사 + 목적어 + to부정사」 형태로 쓸 수 있는 동사들이다.

advise	allow	ask	expect	force	get	invite
order	remind	teach	tell	want	would like	

I **want you to come** to my birthday party. 나는 네가 내 생일파티에 왔으면 좋겠어.
I didn't **expect her to come** this early. 나는 그녀가 이렇게 빨리 오리라고는 예상하지 못했다.
Who **taught you to swim?** 누가 너에게 수영하는 것을 가르쳐줬니?
Please **remind me to call** Ann tomorrow. 내일 Ann에게 전화할 것을 상기시켜줘.

3. 「의문사 + to부정사」

「의문사 + to부정사」는 명사역할을 하면서 문장에서 주로 목적어 역할을 한다. 의문사 중 why를 사용한 「why + to부정사」구문은 쓰지 않는다.

「what+to부정사」 무엇을 ~해야 할지	「how+to부정사」 어떻게 ~해야 할지
「when+to부정사」 언제 ~해야 할지	「where+to부정사」 어디에서 ~해야 할지
「who(m)+to부정사」 누구와/누구를 ~해야 할지	「whether+to부정사」 ~를 할지 하지말지

I don't know **what to say.** 나는 무엇을 말해야 할지 모르겠다.(=I don't know what I should say.)
Do you know **how to use** this machine? 이 기계를 어떻게 사용해야하는 지 아니? (=Do you know how I should use this machine?)

Unit Test

1. 대화가 자연스럽도록 보기의 단어를 이용하여 「의문사＋to부정사」형태에 맞게 빈칸을 채우시오.

보기 |　get　　ask　　leave　　park　　meet

1. A: I don't know _____ _____ _____ my car.
   B: You can park behind the building.
2. A: Could you tell me _____ _____ _____ to the nearest bank?
   B: Go straight for three blocks and it's on your right.
3. A: I don't know _____ _____ _____ this question to.
   B: Ask David. He might know something about it.
4. A: Do you know _____ _____ _____?
   B: I think it's around 8:00.
5. A: I can't decide _____ _____ _____ him or not.
   B: Go and meet him. He's been waiting for you for a long time.

2. 우리말과 일치하도록 괄호 안의 단어를 알맞게 배열하시오.

1. 나는 매니저를 만나고 싶어요. (to/ want/ I/ see the manager)

   _____

2. 나는 네 소식을 듣고 싶다. (hope/ I/ hear from you/ to)

   _____

3. 우리는 그녀가 이렇게 일찍 떠나리라 예상하지 못했다. (didn't/ we/ her/ expect/ to leave this early)

   _____

4. 나는 네가 내 말을 들었으면 좋겠어. (want/ to listen to me/ I/ you)

   _____

5. 나는 누구를 초대해야 할 지 모르겠어. (who/ I don't know/ to invite)

   _____

6. 내가 어떻게 내 발음을 향상시킬 수 있는지 말해봐. (to improve my pronunciation/ how/ tell me)

   _____

7. 나는 무슨 말을 할지 모르겠어. (to say/ I don't know/ what)

   _____

8. 그녀의 편지에 답장을 해야 할 지 결정 못하겠어. (whether/ I can't decide/ to answer her letter)

   _____

Writing Pattern Practice | 동사＋to부정사, 동사＋목적어＋to부정사, 의문사＋to부정사

Pattern 1_ 「동사 + to부정사」

agree	ask	decide	expect	hope	plan
refuse	want	wish	would like	would prefer	

나는 혼자 가기를 원한다. _____

나는 네 소식을 듣고 싶다.(hope to hear) _____

우리는 늦을 거라고 예상했다. _____

우리는 유럽으로 갈 계획이다.(I'm planning~) _____

Pattern 2_ 「동사 + 목적어 + to부정사」

advise	allow	ask	expect	force	get	invite
order	remind	teach	tell	want	would like	

나는 네가 내 생일파티에 왔으면 좋겠어.(want) _____

나는 그녀가 이렇게 빨리 오리라고는 예상하지 못했다.(this early)

_____

누가 너에게 수영하는 것을 가르쳐줬니? _____

나는 Jane에게 더 조심하라고 부탁했다.(ask) _____

나는 여동생에게 커피를 사올 것을 상기시켰다.(remind) _____

누가 너에게 식사값을 지불하라고 했니?(ask, pay for the meal)

_____

Pattern 3_ 「의문사 + to부정사」

「what+to부정사」 무엇을 ～해야 할지	「how+to부정사」 어떻게 ～해야 할지
「when+to부정사」 언제 ～해야 할지	「where+to부정사」 어디에서 ～해야 할지
「who(m)+to부정사」 누구와/누구를 ～해야 할지	「whether+to부정사」 ～를 할지 하지말지

나는 무엇을 먹어야 할지 모르겠다. _____

너는 이 기계를 어떻게 사용해야하는 지 아니? _____

나는 누구를 초대해야 할 지 모르겠어. _____

그녀의 편지에 답장을 해야 할 지 결정 못하겠어. _____

44

49 to부정사를 이용한 다양한 표현

● Pattern   to + 동사원형

A: Come on in. It's nice to see you again.
B: I'm happy to be here.
A: Would you care for a drink?
B: A glass of water would be fine.

1. 「형용사 + to + 동사원형」

형용사 뒤에 쓰이는 to부정사는 보통 형용사를 꾸며주는 부사 역할을 한다. 부정사와 자주 쓰이는 형용사들은 다음과 같다.

nice	glad	pleased	sorry	afraid
lucky	likely	willing	ready	eager(간절히 원하는)

It was **nice to hear** from you. 네 소식을 듣게 되어 반가웠어.
I was **glad to see** you. 너를 봐서 반가웠어.
They were **pleased to be** going home. 그들은 집에 가게 되어 기뻤다.
I was **sorry to call** so late. 너무 늦게 전화해서 미안했어.
Are you **afraid to be** alone in the dark? 어둠속에 혼자 있는 것이 두렵니?
He was incredibly **lucky to be** alive. 그는 정말 운 좋게 살아남았다.
It's **likely to rain.** 비가 올 것 같다.
I'm **willing to see** you soon. 곧 너를 기꺼이 보고 싶다.
Are you **ready to order?** 주문할 준비 되셨습니까?
She was very **eager to meet** me. 그녀는 나를 만나기를 간절히 원했다.

2. 「명사 + to + 동사원형」

명사 뒤에 쓰이는 to부정사는 보통 그 명사를 꾸며주는 형용사 역할을 한다. 그리고 이 때 「명사 +to부정사+전치사」의 형태로 쓰는 경우는 명사가 전치사의 목적어 역할을 하는 경우이다.
Would you like **something to drink?** 마실 것 좀 드릴까요?
Do you need **something to write with?** 쓸 것이(필기도구) 필요하세요?
I think you need **someone to count on.** 너는 믿고 의지할 사람이 필요한 것 같아.

3. 「in order to + 동사원형」

「in order to~」는 '~하기 위하여' 라는 목적을 나타내는 표현으로 주로 일상생활에서는 in order 를 생략하고 to부정사만 쓴다. (in order) to는 「so that + 주어 + can(could)/won't(wouldn't)~」 과 바꿔 쓸 수 있다.

I sat down **(in order) to rest.** 나는 쉬려고 앉았다. (=I sat down **so that I could rest**.)

I studied English **(in order) to have** a better chance of getting a job. 나는 좀 더 좋은 직장을 구할 수 있는 기회를 얻으려고 영어를 공부했다. (=I studied English **so that I could have** a better chance of getting a job.)

We kept quiet **(in order) not to wake** her up. 우리는 그녀를 깨우지 않기 위해 조용히 있었다. (=We kept quiet **so that we wouldn't wake** her up.)

4. 「too + 형용사/부사 + to + 동사원형」

'너무 ~해서 …할 수 없다' 라는 뜻으로 「so + 형용사/부사 + that + 주어 + can't/couldn't~」으로 바꿔 쓸 수 있다.

I was **too tired to finish** my work. 나는 너무 피곤해서 일을 끝마칠 수 없었다. (=I was **so tired that I couldn't finish** my work.)

They spoke **too fast** for us **to understand.** 그들은 우리가 이해하기에 너무 빨리 말했다. (=They spoke **so fast that we couldn't understand.**)

5. 「형용사/부사 + enough + to + 동사원형」

'~하기에 충분히 …하다' 라는 뜻으로 「so + 형용사/부사 + that + 주어 + can/could~」로 바꿔 쓸 수 있다.

Sally is **old enough to do** what she wants. Sally는 자신이 원하는 것을 할 수 있을 만큼 충분히 나이를 먹었다 (=Sally is **so old that she can do** what she wants.)

Benny was **experienced enough to do** the job. Benny는 그 일을 하기에 충분한 경력이 있었다. (=Benny was **so experienced that he** could do the job.)

6. 「the last + 명사 + to + 동사원형」

'~할 마지막 …이다,' 즉 '결코 ~하지 않을 …이다' 라는 뜻이다.

Shiela is **the last one to know** the truth. Shiela는 진실을 알 마지막 사람이다.→Shiela는 진실을 결코 모를 사람이다.

Tom is **the last one to tell** a lie. Tom은 거짓말을 할 마지막 사람이다.→Tom은 결코 거짓말을 할 사람이 아니다.

Unit Test

1. 빈칸에 알맞은 말을 「to + 동사원형」 형태로 써 넣으시오.

1. 네 소식을 듣게 되어 반가웠어.→ It was nice _____ _____ from you.
2. 너를 봐서 반가웠어. → I was glad _____ _____ you.
3. 늦게 전화해서 미안했어. → I was sorry _____ _____ so late.
4. 너는 어둠 속에 혼자 있는 것이 두렵니? → Are you afraid _____ _____ alone in the dark?
5. 눈이 올 것 같다. → It's likely _____ _____.
6. 마실 것 좀 드릴까요? → Would you like something _____ _____?

2. 다음 문장을 「so that + 주어 + can(could)/won't(wouldn't)~」 형태로 바꿔 쓰시오.

1. I sat down (in order) to rest.

→ _____

2. I kept quiet (in order) not to bother my dad.

→ _____

3. 다음 문장을 「so + 형용사/부사 + that + 주어 + can't/couldn't~」 형태로 바꿔 쓰시오.

1. She's too young to get married.

→ _____

2. The food was too hot to eat.

→ _____

3. They spoke too fast for us to understand.

→ _____

4. 다음 문장을 「so + 형용사/부사 + that + 주어 + can/could~」 형태로 바꿔 쓰시오.

1. Those apples are ripe enough to eat.

→ _____

2. She's rich enough to buy a BMW.

→ _____

3. He was experienced enough to do the job.

→ _____

5. 우리말과 일치하도록 괄호 안의 단어를 알맞게 배열하시오.

1. 그녀는 진실을 알 마지막 사람이다. (the last one/ she's/ to know the truth)

→ _____

2. 그는 거짓말을 할 마지막 사람이다. (the last one/ to tell a lie/ he's)

→ _____

Writing Pattern Practice | to부정사를 이용한 다양한 표현

Pattern 1_ 「형용사 + to + 동사원형」

네 소식을 듣게 되어 반가웠어.(nice) _____

내가 너무 늦게 전화해서 미안했어.(so late) _____

당신은 해고 당하지 않아서 다행이었어.(lucky, be fired) _____

_____

비가 올 것 같다.(likely) _____

나는 곧 너를 기꺼이 보고 싶다.(willing) _____

너는 나갈 준비 되었니? _____

Pattern 2_ 「명사 + to + 동사원형」

마실 것 좀 드릴까요?(Would you like~) _____

당신은 쓸 것이(필기도구) 필요하세요? _____

Pattern 3_ 「(in order) to + 동사원형」 = 「so that ~can(could)/won't(wouldn't)」

그들은 뉴욕에 직장을 구하러 왔다.(look for) _____

우리는 그녀를 방해하지 않기 위해 조용히 있었다.(keep quiet, bother) _____

_____

Pattern 4_ 「too + 형용사/부사 + to + 동사원형」 = 「so + 형용사/부사 + that + 주어 + can't/couldn't~」

나는 너무 피곤해서 일 하러 갈 수 없었다. _____

그들은 우리가 이해하기에 너무 빨리 말했다.(fast) _____

Pattern 5_ 「형용사/부사 + enough + to + 동사원형」 = 「so + 형용사/부사 + that + 주어 + can/could~」

Sally는 그 영화를 보기에 충분히 나이를 먹었다. _____

Benny는 그 일을 하기에 충분히 경력이 있었다. _____

Pattern 6_ 「the last + 명사 + to + 동사원형」

Shiela는 진실을 알 마지막 사람이다.(one) _____

Tom은 거짓말을 할 마지막 사람이다.(one) _____

50 동명사

● **Pattern**   동사+ing : 명사역할

Grammar in Practice

A: What would you like to do? I think seeing a movie would be fun.
B: Thank you for asking, but I'm not in the mood.
A: Come on. It would do you good to go out.
B: No, I want to stay home tonight.

Grammar in Use

1. **동명사 「동사+ing」의 쓰임**

동명사는 동사의 성질을 가지고 있으면서 문장 안에서 명사 역할을 한다.

1. 주어 역할

   Seeing a movie is fun. 영화 보는 것은 재미있다.

2. 목적어 역할

   I enjoy **seeing a movie.** 나는 영화 보는 것을 좋아한다.

   I MORE TIPS I 5형식 「주어+동사+목적어+목적보어」에서 동명사가 목적어로 쓰일 경우 보통 가목적어 it을 사용한다.
   I found it difficult **learning** a second language. 나는 제2외국어를 배우는 것이 어렵다는 것을 알게 되었다.

3. 보어 역할

   My hobby is **seeing a movie.** 내 취미는 영화 보는 것이다.

4. 전치사의 목적어 역할

   I feel like **seeing a movie.** 나는 (지금) 영화 보고 싶다.

2. **동명사의 완료시제 「having + 과거분사」**

완료시제는 본동사보다 과거의 사실을 말할 때 쓴다.
I'm ashamed of **having been** rude. 나는 무례하게 군 것이 부끄럽다.
He admitted **having robbed** the bank. 그는 은행을 턴 것을 시인했다.

3. **동명사의 부정**

동명사 앞에 not, never 등의 부정어를 쓴다.
Would you mind **not turning** on the TV? TV를 켜지 말아 주시겠어요?
Jerry is angry about **not having** been invited. Jerry는 초대받지 못한 것에 대해 화가 나있다.
I'm proud of **never having** cheated before. 나는 커닝을 해보지 않은 것이 자랑스럽다.

4. 행위자를 나타내는 표현

1. 의미상의 주어를 밝히는 경우

동명사의 의미상 주어가 명사/ 대명사일 경우 소유격, 목적격 모두 사용한다. 보통 목적격을 사용할 경우 더 가벼운 표현이 되며(less formal) 의미상 주어가 무생물 명사일 경우 목적격을 사용한다는 점을 유의한다. 그리고 동사가 지각동사(see, hear, watch, feel 등)일 경우도 목적격을 주로 사용한다.

● 의미상 주어로 소유격 사용

Does **my smoking** annoy you? 제가 담배 피워서 짜증나세요?

I was upset about **Sarah's trying** to lie to me. 나는 Sarah가 거짓말하려고 해서 화가 났다.

● 의미상 주어로 목적격 사용

Do you mind **me coming in?** 제가 들어가도 될까요?

We're sure of **the rumor being** true. 우리는 그 소문이 사실일 것이라고 확신한다.

I saw **him getting** off the bus. (hear, watch, feel 등) 나는 그가 버스에서 내리는 것을 봤다.

2. 의미상의 주어를 밝히지 않는 경우

● 의미상의 주어가 주어나 목적어와 일치하는 경우

I feel like <u>my(X)</u> **going** for a walk. 나는 산책하고 싶다.

● 의미상의 주어가 일반인 주어일 경우

<u>Our(X)</u> **Exercising** everyday is good for health. 매일 운동하는 것은 네 건강에 좋다.

● 누구나 알 수 있는 주어일 경우

Thank you for <u>your(X)</u> **coming.** 와줘서 고마워.

Unit Test

1. 다음 밑줄 친 것이 동명사이면 '동' 현재분사이면 '분' 이라고 쓰시오.

   1. My job is pretty <u>boring</u>. (   )
   2. Do you mind me <u>asking</u> you a question? (   )
   3. <u>Smoking</u> cigarettes is bad for you. (   )
   4. I hate <u>saying</u> goodbye. (   )
   5. Jack's lessons are always <u>interesting</u>. (   )
   6. I find this job very <u>tiring</u>. (   )
   7. What's all this <u>shouting</u>? (   )
   8. I can't not stand your <u>telling</u> me what to do. (   )
   9. It was an <u>exciting</u> new challenge. (   )
   10. John was upset about my <u>leaving</u> too early. (   )

2. 다음 밑줄 친 부분이 주어역할을 하면 '주', 목적어역할을 하면 '목', 보어역할을 하면 '보', 전치사의 목적어 역할을 하면 '전' 이라고 쓰시오.

   1. I hate <u>packing</u>. (   )
   2. <u>Learning</u> languages is difficult. (   )
   3. My dream is <u>becoming</u> a professor. (   )
   4. Are you interested in <u>bowling</u>? (   )
   5. The president went on <u>talking</u> for hours. (   )
   6. He denied <u>stealing</u> the money. (   )
   7. Do you enjoy <u>meeting</u> people? (   )
   8. My favorite sports are <u>skiing</u> and <u>playing</u> tennis. (   )
   9. <u>Drinking</u> too much alcohol is bad for your health. (   )
   10. I feel like <u>going</u> out. (   )

3. 우리말과 일치하도록 괄호 안의 단어를 알맞게 배열하시오.

   1. 제가 담배 피워서 짜증나세요? (my smoking/ does/ annoy you/ ?)

   _____

   2. 제가 들어가도 될까요? (coming in/ do you/ mind me/ ?)

   _____

   3. 그 파티는 David이 집에 일찍 가야 하는 것 때문에 망쳐졌다.
      (by David's / was ruined/ the party/ having to go home early)

   _____

   4. 나는 그가 버스에 오르는 것을 봤다. (I/ getting on the bus/ saw him)

   _____

Writing Pattern Practice | 동명사

Pattern 1_ 「동사-ing」 동명사의 명사역할

여행하는 것은 재미있다.(travel) _____

나는 여행하는 것을 좋아한다. _____

내 취미는 여행하는 것이다. _____

나는 (지금) 여행하고 싶다.(feel like) _____

Pattern 2_ 「having + 과거분사」 동명사의 완료시제

나는 무례하게 군 것이 부끄럽다.(I'm ashamed of~, be rude)

_____

그녀는 CD player를 고장낸 것을 시인했다.(admit, break)

_____

Pattern 3_ 「not, never + 동사-ing」 동명사의 부정

TV를 켜지 말아 주시겠어요?(Would you mind~) _____

나는 전에 커닝을 해보지 않은 것이 자랑스럽다.(I'm proud of~, never)

_____

Pattern 4_ 「소유격 + 동명사」 의미상 주어로 소유격 사용

제가 담배 피워서 짜증나세요?(annoy) _____

나는 Sarah가 거짓말하려고 해서 화가 났다.(upset about, try to lie)

_____

Pattern 5_ 「목적격 + 동명사」 의미상 주어로 목적격 사용

제가 들어가도 될까요?(Do you mind~) _____

우리는 그 소문이 사실일 것이라고 확신한다.(We're sure of~)

_____

나는 그가 버스에서 내리는 것을 봤다.(get off) _____

Pattern 6_ 의미상의 주어를 밝히지 않는 경우

나는 산책하고 싶다.(feel like, go for a walk) _____

덜 먹는 것이 네 건강에 좋다.(eat less) _____

기다려줘서 고마워. _____

51 동사 + 동명사, 동사 + 목적어 + 동명사

● Pattern   동사 + 동사ㅏing,

동사 + 목적어 + 동사ㅏing

Grammar in Practice

(At the movie theater)

A: Have you seen that move?

B: Yes, but I don't mind watching it twice.

A: Are you sure?

B: Absolutely. It's really worth seeing it again. I can't wait for it to be released on DVD.

Grammar in Use

1. 「동사 + 동사ㅏing」

다음은 동명사를 목적어로 갖는 동사들이다.

admit	appreciate	avoid	consider	delay
deny	dislike	enjoy	finish	forgive
give up	(can't) help	imagine	keep (on)	mind
suggest	(can't) stand	postpone(put off)		

I **enjoy cooking.** 나는 요리하는 것을 즐긴다.

He's **finished repairing** his car. 그는 차 수리하는 것을 끝마쳤다.

My uncle has **given up smoking.** 삼촌은 담배를 끊으셨다.

I **can't help falling** in love with you. 나는 너와 사랑에 빠지지 않을 수 없다.

The doctor **suggested taking** a long holiday. 의사선생님이 긴 여행을 떠나라고 제안하셨다.

2. 「동사 + 목적어 + 동사ㅏing」

다음은 「동사 + 목적어 + 동명사」 형태를 취하는 동사들이다.

dislike	imagine	stop	spend	see	stop/prevent~(from)

I **dislike people telling** a lie. 나는 사람들이 거짓말하는 것을 싫어한다.

I can't **imagine him cooking.** 나는 그가 요리하는 것을 상상할 수 없다.

My grandpa **spends all his time gardening.** 할아버지는 정원일 하면서 모든 시간을 보내신다.

I **saw him getting** out of the car. 나는 그가 차에서 내리는 것을 봤다.

This treatment will **prevent cancer (from) developing.** 이 치료가 암의 진행을 막을 것입니다.

4. 「동사 + to부정사」와 「동사 + 동명사」의 비교

* 동사가 to부정사 또는 동명사를 모두 목적어로 취할 수 있는 경우

의미차이가 거의 없음	like, love, prefer, hate, begin, start, continue 등	It **started raining(=to rain)** again. 또 비가 오기 시작했다. I **hate packing(=to pack)** suitcase. 나는 가방 꾸리는 것을 싫어한다.
의미차이가 있음	● **try** try to ~하기 위해 노력하다 try ~ing ~를 시험삼아 해보다	I **tried to finish** it as quickly as I could. 나는 가능한 빨리 그것을 끝마치기 위해 노력했다. Why don't we **try pushing** this car together? 우리 같이 이 차를 밀어보면 어떨까?
	● **remember** remember to ~할 것을 기억하다 remember ~ing ~한 것을 기억하다	I **remember buying** my first bicycle. 나는 처음 자전거를 샀을 때를 기억한다. **Remember to** e-mail me. 나에게 이메일 보낼 것을 기억해라.
	● **forget** forget to ~할 것을 잊다 forget ~ing ~한 것을 잊다	I **forgot to** call Larry. 나는 Larry에게 전화할 것을 잊어버렸다. I will never **forget meeting** you. 나는 너를 만났던 것을 잊지 못할 거야.
	● **go on** go on to ~에 이어 (다른 것을) 계속하다 go on ~ing ~(한가지 일)을 계속하다	Sally **went on to talk** about her other problems. Sally는 그녀의 다른 문제들에 대해서 계속 얘기했다. Cindy **went on talking** about her boyfriend for hours. Cindy는 그녀의 남자친구에 대해서 계속 이야기 했다.
	● **need** need to ~를 할 필요가 있다 (능동의 의미) need ~ing ~될 필요가 있다 (수동의 의미)	You **need to get** more exercise. 너는 운동을 더 할 필요가 있다. This tire **needs changing.** 이 타이어는 교체될 필요가 있다. (=This tire **needs to be changed.**)
	● **deserve** deserve to ~할 자격이 있다 (능동의 의미) deserve ~ing ~될 자격이 있다 (수동의 의미)	He **deserves to get** all As. 그는 전부 A를 받을 자격이 있다. I don't think his article **deserves reading.** 그의 기사가 읽혀질 가치가 있다고 생각하지 않는다. (=I don't think his article **deserves to be read.**)
	● **stop** stop to ~하기 위해 멈추다 stop ~ing ~하는 것을 멈추다	I **stopped to rest.** 나는 쉬려고 멈췄다. I **stopped running.** 나는 뛰는 것을 멈추었다.

Unit Test

1. 다음 보기에서 주로 동명사를 목적어로 갖는 동사를 모두 골라 동그라미 하시오.

보기	agree	avoid	can't help	fail	hope	put off	enjoy
	suggest	ask	decide	mind	expect	consider	

2. 다음 보기에서 to부정사 또는 동명사를 목적어로 취해도 의미의 차이가 거의 없는 동사를 모두 골라 동그라미 하시오.

보기	prefer	remember	hate	begin	forget
	go on	start	continue	try	stop

3. 우리말과 일치하도록 괄호 안의 단어를 알맞게 배열하시오.

1. 그녀는 동물원에 가는 것을 제안했다. (she suggested/ to the zoo/ going)

2. 빵 좀 건네주시겠어요? (passing/ mind/ would you/ the bread/ ?)

3. 나는 그가 춤추는 것 상상할 수 없다. (dancing/ I can't/ him / imagine)

4. 아무도 그가 원하는 것을 하는 것을 막을 수 없다. (stop/ him/ nobody can/ what he wants to/ doing)

5. 또 비가 오기 시작했다. (started/ it/ raining again)

6. 나는 문을 잠그는 것을 잊었다. (forgot to/ lock the door/ I)

7. 그는 그의 모든 시간을 잠자면서 보냈다. (sleeping/ spent/ all his time/ he)

8. 그는 그의 일에 관해서 계속 이야기 했다. (went on/ he/ talking about his job)

9. 이 차는 서비스 받을 필요가 있다. (this car/ servicing/ needs)

10. 나는 걸음을 멈췄다. (I/ walking/ stopped)

Writing Pattern Practice | 동사 + 동명사, 동사 + 목적어 + 동명사

admit	appreciate	avoid	consider	delay	deny	dislike
enjoy	finish	forgive	give up	(can't) help	imagine	(can't) stand
mind	suggest	keep (on)	postpone(put off)			

나는 요리하는 것을 즐긴다. _____

그는 차 수리하는 것을 끝마쳤다.(He has~, repair)_____

삼촌은 담배를 끊으셨다.(My uncle has given up~) _____

나는 너와 사랑에 빠지지 않을 수 없다. _____

의사선생님이 긴 여행을 떠나라고 제안하셨다.(take a long holiday) _____

너는 내가 말하고 있을 때 계속 끼어들어.(interrupt, talk) _____

dislike	imagine	stop	spend	see	stop/prevent~(from)

나는 사람들이 거짓말하는 것을 싫어한다.(dislike) _____

나는 그가 요리하는 것을 상상할 수 없다. _____

할아버지는 정원일 하면서 모든 시간을 보내신다.(all his time, garden) _____

나는 그가 차에서 내리는 것을 봤다.(get out of) _____

이 치료가 암의 진행을 막을 것입니다.(This treatment~, develop) _____

나는 빗속을 걷는 것을 좋아한다. _____

또 비가 오기 시작했다.(It started~) _____

56

Pattern 4_ 「동사 + to부정사」와 「동사 + 동명사」가 의미가 다른 경우
try, remember, forget, go on, need, deserve, stop + 동명사/ to부정사

나는 가능한 빨리 그것을 끝마치기 위해 노력했다.(~as quickly as I could.)

_____

우리 같이 이 차를 밀어보면 어떨까?(Why don't we~)

_____

나는 처음 자전거를 샀을 때를 기억한다.(my first bicycle) _____

나에게 이메일 보낼 것을 기억해라.(e-mail) _____

나는 Larry에게 전화할 것을 잊어버렸다. _____

나는 너를 만났던 것을 절대 잊지 못할 거야. _____

Sally는 그녀의 다른 문제들에 대해서 계속 얘기했다.(Sally went on to~)

_____

Cindy는 그녀의 남자친구에 대해서 몇 시간동안 이야기 했다.(for hours)

_____

너는 운동을 더 할 필요가 있다.(get) _____

이 타이어는 교체될 필요가 있다.(changing) _____

그는 전부 A를 받을 자격이 있다.(get all As) _____

그의 기사가 읽혀질 가치가 있다고 생각하지 않는다.(I don't think~)

_____

나는 쉬려고 멈췄다.(rest) _____

나는 뛰는 것을 멈추었다. _____

52 동명사를 이용한 다양한 표현

● Pattern   동사+ing

A: I haven't seen you for a long time. How have you been?
B: I've been busy working.
A: How's your new job?
B: Not bad. I'm getting used to it.

동명사를 포함하는 관용적인 표현을 숙어처럼 익혀두자.

1. 「There is no ~ing」 ~하는 것은 불가능하다 (=It is impossible to~)
   There is no telling what will happen in the future. 미래에 일어날 일을 말한다는 것은
   불가능하다. (=It is impossible to tell what will happen in the future.)

2. 「It is no use ~ing」 ~해도 소용없다
   It is no use crying over spilt milk. 엎질러진 우유를 놓고 울어봤자 소용없다.

3. 「cannot help ~ing」 ~하지 않을 수 없다 (=cannot but + 동사원형)
   I cannot help falling in love with you. 나는 너와 사랑에 빠지지 않을 수 없다.
   (=I cannot but fall in love with you.)

4. 「be busy (in) ~ing」 ~하느라 바쁘다
   I've **been busy working.** (그동안) 일하느라 바빴다.

5. 「feel like ~ing」 ~하고 싶다
   I **feel like throwing** up. 토할 것 같다.
   I don't **feel like going** out tonight. 오늘 밤엔 외출할 기분이 나질 않는다.

6. 「go ~ing」 ~하러 가다
   Let's **go hiking.** 등산(하이킹) 가자.   Let's **go dancing.** 춤추러 가자.
   Let's **go fishing.** 낚시하러 가자.   Let's **go skiing.** 스키타러 가자.
   Let's **go skating.** 스케이트 타러 가자.   Let's **go drinking.** 술 마시러 가자.
   Let's **go bowling.** 볼링 치러 가자.   Let's **go eating.** 먹으러 가자.

7. 「look forward to ~ing」 ~하기를 손꼽아 기다리다
   I **look forward to seeing** you. 뵙기를 손 꼽아 기다릴께요.

8. 「get(=be) used to ~ing」 ~에 익숙해지다 (=get(=be) accustomed to~)

I **got used to driving** a car after dark. 나는 저녁에 운전하는데 익숙해졌다

(=I got accustomed to driving a car after dark.)

I**'m not used to** living in Seoul. 나는 서울에 사는 것에 익숙하지 않다.

(=I'm not accustomed to living in Seoul.)

9. 「object to ~ing」 ~하는 것을 반대하다

Do you **object to working** on Saturdays? 당신은 토요일 근무를 반대합니까?

10. 「have trouble ~ing」 ~에 문제가 있다

Did you **have any trouble getting** a visa? 비자를 받는데 문제가 있었니?

I don't think they **have trouble finding** this place. 그들이 이 곳을 찾는데 문제가 있을 것 같지 않다.

11. 「be worth ~ing」 ~할 가치가 있다

France **is worth visiting.** 프랑스는 방문할 가치가 있다.

Whatever **is worth doing** at all is worth doing well. 〈속담〉 할 만한 일이라면 훌륭히 할 만한 가치가 있다.

12. 「What do you say to~?」 ~하는 게 어때? (=How about ~ing?)

What do you say to going on a picnic? 피크닉 가는 게 어때?

(=How about going on a picnic?)

13. 「On ~ing」 ~하자마자 (=As soon as 주어 + 동사)

On seeing the police officer, he ran away. 경찰관을 보자마자 그는 도망갔다.

(=As soon as he saw the police officer, he ran away.)

14. 「not(never) … without ~ing」 ~하지 않고는 …하지 않는다

You **can't** make an omelette **without breaking** eggs. 〈속담〉 달걀을 깨지 않고 오믈렛을 만들 수는 없다.(희생없이 목적을 달성할 수 없다.)

15. 「need ~ing」 ~될 필요가 있다 (=need to be pp: 수동의 의미)

This car **needs washing.** 이 차는 세차되어야 한다. (=This car needs to be washed.)

Your shoes **need mending.** 네 신발은 수선되어야 한다. (=Your shoes need to be mended.)

Your hair **needs cutting.** 네 머리는 잘려져야 한다. (=Your hair needs to be cut.)

I don't think his book **needs reading.** 그의 책이 읽혀질 필요가 있다고 생각하지 않는다. (=I don't think his book needs to be read.)

Unit Test

1. 다음 두 문장이 같은 뜻이 되도록 빈칸에 알맞은 말을 써 넣으시오.

1. It is impossible to tell what will happen in the future.
   = There _____ _____ telling what will happen in the future.
2. She could not but congratulate him.
   = She _____ _____ _____ congratulating him.
3. I got accustomed to driving a car on the left.
   = I got _____ _____ driving a car on the left.
4. How about seeing a movie?
   = _____ _____ _____ _____ to seeing a movie?
5. As soon as he saw me, he walked away.
   = _____ seeing me, he walked away.

2. 우리말과 일치하도록 괄호 안의 단어를 알맞게 배열하시오.

1. 엎질러진 우유를 놓고 울어봤자 소용없다. (over spilt milk/ crying/ it is no use)

   _____

2. 나는 웃을 수 밖에 없었다. (laughing/ couldn't/ help/ I)

   _____

3. 나는 공부하느라 바쁘다. (busy/ I'm/ studying)

   _____

4. 피자 먹고 싶다. (eating pizza/ feel like/ I)

   _____

5. 춤추러 가자. (go/ let's/ dancing)

   _____

6. 우리는 당신의 연락을 기다리겠습니다. (look forward to/ hearing from you/ we)

   _____

7. 나는 네가 Alice와 결혼하는 것 반대야. (your marrying Alice/ object to/ I)

   _____

8. 너는 비자를 받는데 문제가 있었니? (have any trouble/ did you/ getting a visa/ ?)

   _____

9. 이 책은 읽을 만한 가치가 있다. (this book/ reading/ is worth)

   _____

10. 네 신발은 수선되어야 한다. (your shoes/ mending/ need)

   _____

Writing Pattern Practice | 동명사를 이용한 다양한 표현

Pattern 1_ 「There is no ~ing」 ~하는 것은 불가능하다

미래에 일어날 일을 말한다는 것은 불가능하다.(tell) _____

Pattern 2_ 「It is no use ~ing」 ~해도 소용없다

엎질러진 우유를 놓고 울어봤자 소용없다. _____

그것에 대해 논쟁해봤자 소용없다.(argue) _____

Pattern 3_ 「cannot help ~ing」 ~하지 않을 수 없다

나는 웃지 않을 수 없었다.(laugh) _____

나는 궁금해하지 않을 수 없었다.(wonder) _____

Pattern 4_ 「be busy (in) ~ing」 ~하느라 바쁘다

나는 청소하느라 바빴다. _____

그 비서는 전화받느라 바쁘다.(answer, phone calls) _____

Pattern 5_ 「feel like ~ing」 ~하고 싶다

나는 토할 것 같았다. _____

나는 저녁 먹으러 나가고 싶다.(for dinner) _____

Pattern 6_ 「go ~ing」 ~하러 가다

등산(하이킹) 가자. _____

Pattern 7_ 「look forward to ~ing」 ~하기를 손꼽아 기다리다

당신을 뵙기를 손꼽아 기다릴께요.(see) _____

Pattern 8_ 「get(=be) used to ~ing」 ~에 익숙해지다

나는 서울에 사는 것에 익숙해졌다. _____

나는 그녀가 늦는 것에 익숙해졌다.(I've got~, her) _____

Pattern 9_ 「object to」 ~하는 것을 반대하다

당신은 토요일 근무를 반대합니까? _____

Pattern 10_ 「have trouble ~ing」 ~에 문제가 있다

그들이 이 곳을 찾는데 문제가 있을 것 같지 않다.(I don't think they~)

_____

Pattern 11_ 「be worth ~ing」 ~할 가치가 있다

프랑스는 방문할 가치가 있다.

_____

Pattern 12_ 「What do you say to~?」 ~하는 게 어때?

외식하는 게 어때?(eat out)

_____

Pattern 13_ 「On ~ing」 ~하자마자 (=As soon as 주어 + 동사)

나를 보자마자 그는 도망갔다.

_____

Pattern 14_ 「not(never) … without ~ing」 ~하지 않고는 …하지 않는다

달걀을 깨지 않고 오믈렛을 만들 수는 없다.(You can't~, break eggs)

_____

Pattern 15_ 「need ~ing」 ~될 필요가 있다

내 구두는 닦여져야 한다.(shine)

_____

네 머리는 잘려져야 한다.

_____

1. 둘 중 어법에 알맞은 것을 고르시오.

1. I was (surprising/ surprised) to see Janet there.
2. I find this work very (tiring/ tired).
3. We were (shocking/ shocked) to hear about your grandpa.
4. Do you ever get (boring/ bored) at work?
5. I always keep my room (locking/ locked).
6. The car (parking/ parked) over there is Mike's.
7. Look at the boy (wearing/ worn) a hat.
8. Do you like (mashing/ mashed) potatoes?
9. I saw the tree (cutting/ cut) down.
10. "How would you like your eggs?" "(Scrambling/ Scrambled) eggs, please."

2. 다음 두 문장을 보기와 같이 −ing 또는 Not −ing로 시작하는 분사구문으로 고쳐 쓰시오.

| 보기 | I was hungry. So I ate it all.
→ Being hungry, I ate it all. |

1. I felt sleepy. So I went to bed.
→
2. He's a foreigner. So he needs to practice English.
→
3. I didn't know his phone number. So I wasn't able to contact him.
→
4. We ran out of money. So we couldn't afford to travel to Europe.
→
5. They didn't get here on time. So they couldn't make it to the first class.
→

3. 다음 두 문장을 보기와 같이 Having으로 시작하는 분사구문으로 고쳐 쓰시오.

| 보기 | She finished her homework. Then she went to bed.
→ Having finished her homework, she went to bed. |

1. We saved some money. Then we bought a car.
→
2. After Nancy had taken a shower, she got dressed.
→

4. 다음 문장을 수동태 문장으로 바꾸시오.

1. Everybody loves children.
→ _____

2. Do it.
→ Let _____

3. Sally is looking after her son.
→ _____

4. My mother made me this cake.
→ This cake _____

5. My boss made me work overtime.
→ I _____

5. 틀린 곳을 찾아 밑줄치고 고쳐 쓰시오.

1. This house is big enough of your family to live in.
→ _____

2. It's difficult of me to get up early.
→ _____

3. It's nice for you to remember my birthday.
→ _____

4. I tried to not bother my father.
→ _____

5. I didn't expect you coming here.
→ _____

6. 다음 괄호 안의 동사를 알맞은 형태로 빈칸에 써 넣으시오.

1. I remembered_____(see) Tom two years ago.
2. Don't forget_____(call) me as soon as you come back.
3. Ted is considering_____(move) to Busan.
4. Would you like_____(drink) some tea?
5. The doctor suggested_____(take) some rest.
6. I hope_____(be) a musician.
7. She's given up_____(smoke).

* 다음 밑줄친 문장과 바꿔 쓸 수 있는 것을 고르시오.

1. <u>I was too tired to finish my work.</u>

① I was too tired that I could finish my work.
② I was tired so that I couldn't finish my work.
③ I was so tired that I couldn't finish my work.
④ I was so tired that I could finish my work.

2. <u>Your English is good enough to be an English teacher.</u>

① Your English is good so that you can be an English teacher.
② Your English is too good that you can be an English teacher.
③ Your English is so good that you can be an English teacher.
④ Your English is so good that you can't be an English teacher.

3. 다음 글을 읽고, 밑줄친 우리말에 해당하는 부분을 영작하시오.

They have a lot of crocodiles in Australia. Elizabeth, a 16-year-old girl, was sitting next to a small river. She was relaxing, <u>그녀의 발을 물에 담근 채로</u> All of a sudden, a crocodile that was over 3 meters long jumped out of the water to kill her. Fortunately, she was able to hold on to the branch of a tree. Her mother saw what was happening and jumped into the water. She tried to pull Elizabeth to safety and the crocodile went away.

with_____ _____ in _____ _____

4. 다음 글을 읽고, 빈칸에 차례로 들어갈 알맞은 말을 고르시오.

Do you eat breakfast? Many people fail _____ a good nutritional breakfast because they are in a hurry in the morning. If you skip breakfast, you will not be able to think and perform your best. Many nutritionists agree that breakfast is the most important meal a day. So it is important that you eat a high protein and high energy meal for breakfast. Don't forget _____ breakfast even though you don't have enough time. Get up ten minutes earlier every morning and eat some breakfast.

① to eat - eating   ② eating - eating
③ to eat - to eat   ④ eating - to eat

* Chapter 6 | 문장 연결하기

Unit

53 시간 전치사

● **Pattern**   전치사＋시간을 나타내는 명사

A: Merry Christmas!
B: The same to you!
A: Are you doing anything special **on** Christmas Day?
B: No, I'll probably just stay home.

---

1. 전치사

전치사의 목적어로는 명사, 대명사, 동명사, 명사절 등이 올 수 있다.

● 「전치사 + 명사」
I'm looking **for** Janet. 나는 Janet을 찾고 있다.

● 「전치사 + 대명사」
A good-looking man sat **by** me. 잘 생긴 남자가 내 옆에 앉았다.

● 「전치사 + 동명사」
I feel **like** going out. 나는 나가고 싶다.

● 「전치사 + 절」
Tell me **about** what happened yesterday. 어제 있었던 일에 대해 말해.

| MORE TIPS | 전치사의 목적어는 주로 전치사 다음에 오지만 상황에 따라 목적어가 전치사 앞에 위치하는 경우도 있다.
1. wh- 의문문일 경우
Who are you waiting **for**? 누구를 기다리고 있어?
2. 부정사 구문일 경우
I need some friends to hang around **with**. 나는 같이 어울릴 친구가 필요하다.
3. 관계사절일 경우
This is the book that I told you **about**. 내가 말했던 책이야.

2. at, in, on

at	in	on
at + 시각(clock time), 공휴일(명절), 짧은 시간	in + 월, 년 계절 비교적 긴 시간	on + 특정한 날(날짜, 요일) 날의 일부분

I usually get up **at** 7 o'clock. 나는 보통 7시에 일어난다.
What do you usually do **at** Thanksgiving? 추수감사절에 주로 뭐 하니?
I was born **in** July. 나는 7월에 태어났다.
I walk my dog **in** the morning. 나는 아침에 개를 산책시킨다.
I'm leaving **on** May 1. 나는 5월 1일에 떠나.

See you **on** Thanksgiving Day. 추수감사절 날에 봐.
We have a meeting **on** Monday morning. 우리는 월요일 아침에 회의가 있어.

| MORE TIPS | next, last, this, each, every, tomorrow, yesterday 등의 말 앞에는 시간 전치사 at, in, on 등을 생략한다.
See you **next** Friday. 다음 금요일에 봐요.
Last Christmas I went to Australia. 지난 크리스마스에 나는 호주에 갔었다.

3. by, until(till)

by	until
'~까지' 라는 기한을 말할 때	'~까지 계속' 이라는 뜻으로 동작이나 상태가 ~까지 지속될 때

This book must be returned **by** January 4. 이 책은 1월 4일까지 반납해야 합니다.
Can I stay **until** this weekend? 주말까지 머물러도 될까?

4. for, during, through

for	during	through
for + 구체적인 숫자를 이용한 기간 '~동안'	during + 행사나 사건 또는 특정 기간 '~동안'	'~동안 내내'

I'll stay here **for** about a week. 나는 여기에 일주일 정도 머무를 거야.
During the weekend someone broke into the building. 주말동안 누가 건물에 침입했다.
*How long ~?에 대한 답일 경우에는 for, When ~?에 대한 답일 경우에는 during을 각각 사용한다고 생각하면 쉽게 이해할 수 있다.
I've been busy all **through** the week. 나는 한주 내내 바빴다.

5. before, after, in, within

before	after	in	within
'~전에'	'~후에'	말하는 시점으로부터 '~후에', '~만에'	'~이내에'

I usually go jogging **before** I go to work. 나는 보통 출근하기 전에 조깅을 한다.
We take a coffee break **after** lunch. 우리는 점심식사 후 커피를 마시며 쉰다.
I'll be there **in** ten minutes. 내가 10분 후에 거기에 갈게.
I hope to get a job **within** the next two months. 나는 두 달 안에 직장을 구하기를 희망한다.

6. since, from

since	from
'~이래 줄곧' 주로 완료시제와 함께 사용	'~로부터' 완료를 제외한 시제와 함께 사용

I've been here **since** the end of June. 나는 6월 말부터 여기에 있었다.
I work **from** 9 to 5. 나는 9시부터 5시까지 일한다.

Unit Test

1. 빈칸에 at, in, on 중 알맞은 전치사를 써 넣고, 전치사가 필요 없으면 X표하시오.

1. I'll see you _____ April 1.
2. The exam is _____ my birthday.
3. I'm not free _____ this Friday.
4. I go jogging _____ everyday.
5. I was born _____ 1972.
6. What do you usually do _____ Christmas?
7. I want you to come over to my place _____ my birthday.
8. See you _____ tomorrow.
9. It's very cold _____ January.
10. I saw Susie standing at the bus stop _____ the afternoon.

2. 빈칸에 by, until 중 알맞은 전치사를 써 넣으시오.

1. Can I stay _____ the end of July?
2. She went on crying _____ somebody came.
3. You must use this pork _____ the day after tomorrow.
4. This book must be returned _____ this weekend.
5. You'll just have to wait _____ he's ready to see you.
6. We'll have to leave _____ this evening.
7. You have to finish this work _____ tomorrow.
8. "Can I borrow your book?" " _____ when?"
9. Do you think you can finish painting the fence _____ this afternoon?
10. I'll keep waiting here _____ he shows up.

3. 빈칸에 알맞은 전치사를 보기에서 골라 써 넣으시오.

보기	through	during	in	for

1. 음료수가 쉬는 시간에 제공될 것이다.
   Drinks will be served _____ the interval.
2. 나는 그를 10년 동안 못 봤다.
   I haven't seen him _____ 10 years.
3. 내가 한 시간 후에 거기에 갈게.
   I'll be there _____ an hour.
4. 우리는 밤새 걸었다.
   We walked _____ the night.

Writing Pattern Practice | 시간 전치사

Pattern 1_ 「at, in, on + 명사」

나는 7시에 일어난다.

너는 크리스마스에 주로 뭐 하니?

나는 7월에 태어났다.

나는 5월 1일에 떠나.(I'm leaving~)

우리는 월요일 아침에 회의가 있어.(have)

Pattern 2_ 「by, until(till) + 명사」

우리는 오늘 저녁까지 떠나야 할 거야.(We'll have to~)

내가 주말까지 머물러도 될까?(Can I~?)

Pattern 3_ 「for, during, through + 명사」

나는 여기에 일주일 정도 머무를 거야.

우리는 여름방학동안 하와이에 갔었다.

나는 한주 내내 바빴다.(I've been~)

Pattern 4_ 「before, after, in, within + 명사」

네가 잠자리에 들기 전에 이를 닦아라.

우리는 점심식사 후 커피를 마시며 쉰다.(take a coffee break)

내게 삼사일 후에 다시 물어봐.

그는 다음 두 달 안에 돌아올거야.(be back, the next)

Pattern 5_ 「since, from + 명사」

나는 1999년부터 여기에 있었다.(I've been)

나는 9시부터 5시까지 일한다.

54 장소 전치사

● **Pattern** 전치사＋장소를 나타내는 명사

 Grammar in Practice

A: Does this bus go **to** Disneyland?
B: No. You're going the wrong way. You should have taken the Green Line bus. You can get one **at** the next stop.
A: Is it a long ride?
B: Not that long.

 Grammar in Use

다음은 장소, 위치, 또는 운동방향을 나타내는 다양한 전치사들이다.

1. in(into), out of

● in(into) '~안에', '~안으로'　　　　　● out of '~의 밖으로'

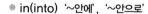　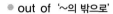

What do you have **in** your hand? 손에 무엇이 있니?
Get **in(into)** the car. 차에 타.
Get **out of** the car. 차에서 내려.

2. at, on, off

● at '~(지점)에'　　　　● on '~(표면) 위에'　　　　● off '~(표면에서) 떨어져'

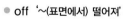

Turn left **at** the crossroads. 사거리에서 좌회전해요.
I sat **on** the chair. 나는 의자에 앉았다.
Take **off** your jacket. 재킷을 벗어.

3. over, above, under, below

● over '~바로 위에'　　　　　　　　● above '~보다 높이', '~위에'

72

● under ‘~바로 아래’

● below ‘~보다 아래’, ‘~아래’

Look at the bridge **over** the river. 강 위에 있는 다리를 봐.
He lifted his hands **above** his head. 그는 그의 손을 머리 위로 들었다.
A boat passed **under** the bridge. 보트가 다리 아래로 지나갔다.
The sun had already sunk **below** the horizon. 해는 이미 수평선 아래로 졌다.

4. by(beside), between, among

● by(beside) ‘옆에’

● between ‘(둘) 사이에’

● among ‘~(셋) 이상 사이에’

Emma was **by** the door. Emma는 문 옆에 있었다.
Come and sit **between** Mary and Sally. 와서 Mary과 Sally사이에 앉아라.
Divide these **among** you three. 이것들을 너희들 셋이 나누어라.

5. from, to, for

● from ‘~로부터’

● to ‘~로’

● for ‘~를 향해’

Are you **from** Canada? 너는 캐나다 출신이니?
I'm going **to** France. 나는 프랑스에 간다.
I'm leaving **for** New York. 나는 뉴욕으로 떠난다.

6. up, down

● up ‘~위로’

● down ‘~아래로’

The sun came **up**. 해가 떴다.
A man came **down** the stairs. 어떤 남자가 계단을 내려왔다.

7. along, across, through

- along '~을 따라서' - across '~건너에', '~을 가로질러' - through '~을 관통하여'

He was walking **along** the street. 그는 거리를 따라 걷고 있었다.
She lives **across** the river 그녀는 강 건너에 산다.
We passed **through** a tunnel. 우리는 터널을 통과했다.

● 중요 장소 전치사 in, at, on			Grammar Point

전치사	영역을 나타내는 in	한 점을 나타내는 at	접촉의 on
쓰임	1. in은 폐쇄되어 있는 공간 안을 나타낼 때 쓴다. Tom is sleeping **in** his room. Tom은 그의 방에서 자고 있다. 2. 도시나 국가 등 비교적 넓은 장소를 나타낼 때 쓴다. I grew up **in** France. 나는 프랑스에서 자랐다. 3. in이 건물 앞에 쓰일 경우 '~안에 있다'는 것을 강조할 때 쓴다. I first met Sam **in** a shop. 나는 Sam을 상점 안에서 처음 만났다. 4. 탈 것과 함께 쓸 경우 작은 교통수단일 때 안으로 들어가는 느낌의 in을 쓴다.(자동차, 택시 등) He got **in** the car. 그는 차에 탔다.	1. at은 어떤 지점을 나타내므로 마을, 건물 등의 대체로 좁은 장소를 나타낼 때 쓴다. Let's meet **at** the club. 클럽에서 만나자. 2. 도시나 국가 등의 넓은 장소일지라도 출발지, 경유지 등의 지점의 뜻으로 쓰였을 경우 at을 쓰기도 한다. Does this train stop **at** Daegu? 이 기차는 대구에 서나요? 3. 건물 앞에 쓰일 경우 건물이 어떤 위치나 지점의 역할을 할 때 쓴다. I'm **at** the post office. 나는 우체국에 있다.	1. on은 표면에 닿은 위에 있을 때 쓴다. There's some bread **on** the table. 테이블 위에 빵이 좀 있다. 2. 탈 것과 함께 쓸 경우 비교적 큰 교통수단이나 위에 올라타는 느낌으로 쓸 때 on을 쓴다.(버스, 기차, 비행기, 배, 자전거, 오토바이, 말 등) There was no room **on** the bus. 버스에는 여유공간이 없었다. I'll go down to the shop **on** my bike. 나는 상점에 자전거를 타고 갈 거야.
in, at, on 과 함께 쓰이는 외워두면 좋은 표현들	in bed in jail (= in prison) in the hospital in the sky in the rain in the sun in the middle of ~ in the distance	at home at work at school at college at the party at the meeting at the traffic light(s) at the door at the window	on the left/ right on the wall on the ceiling on the table on one's stomach(배) on one's back(등) on one's side (옆구리) on the other side of on the spot

Unit Test

1. 다음 그림을 보고 빈칸에 알맞은 전치사를 보기에서 골라 써 넣으시오.

| 보기 | by | out of | in | off | under | on |

1.

What do you have _____ your hand?

2.

He got _____ the car.

3.

I sat _____ the chair.

4.

Take _____ your jacket.

5.

A boat passed _____ the bridge.

6.

Emma was _____ the door.

2. 빈칸에 알맞은 전치사를 보기에서 골라 써 넣으시오.

| 보기 | across   for   down   to |

1. Tom은 학교에 돌아갔다.

   Tome went back _____ school.

2. 그녀는 강 건너에 산다.

   She lives _____ the river.

3. 나는 싱가폴로 떠난다.

   I'm leaving _____ Singapore.

4. 해가 졌다.

   The sun went _____ .

Writing Pattern Practice | 장소 전치사

Pattern 1_ 「in(into), out of + 명사」

네 주머니 안에 무엇이 있니? _____

차에서 내려. _____

Pattern 2_ 「at, on, off + 명사」

신호등에서 멈추세요. _____

나는 마루에 누웠다.(lie-lay-lain) _____

네 모자를 벗어라.(take off) _____

Pattern 3_ 「over, above, under, below + 명사」

강 위에 있는 다리를 봐. _____

그는 그의 손을 머리 위로 들었다.(lift) _____

보트가 다리 아래로 지나갔다. _____

해는 이미 수평선 아래로 졌다.(The sun has~) _____

Pattern 4_ 「by(beside), between, among + 명사」

그녀는 창문 옆에 앉아 있었다.(She was sitting~) _____

와서 Tom과 Mary사이에 앉아라. _____

나무들 사이에 있는 집을 봐라. _____

Pattern 5_ 「from, to, for + 명사」

너는 미국 출신이니? _____

나는 회사에 간다.(walk) _____

그는 부산으로 떠났니? _____

Pattern 6_ 「up, down + 명사」

해가 떴다. _____

어떤 남자가 계단을 내려왔다. _____

Pattern 7_ 「along, across, through + 명사」

그는 거리를 따라 걷고 있었다.(He was walking~) _____

그녀는 강 건너에 산다. _____

우리는 터널을 통과했다.(a tunnel) _____

Unit 55 전치사의 활용

● Pattern 명사+전치사
형용사+전치사
동사+전치사

Grammar in Practice

A: I'm planning on going to ski this weekend. Do you want to come along?
B: Count me in. I care for skiing. Where to?
A: I'm thinking about the nearest ski resort, Yongpyung.
B: That is *terrific!

*terrific 아주 좋은

Grammar in Use

1. 「명사 + 전치사」

● cause of something ~의 원인
Carelessness is often a **cause of** accident. 부주의는 흔히 사고의 원인이 된다.

● reason for something ~의 이유
There is a **reason for** every important thing that happens. 발생하는 중요한 일은 모두 이유가 있다.

● difference between two things ~사이의 차이
There are some **differences between** you and me. 너와 나 사이에는 차이점이 좀 있다.

● relationship with somebody/ something ~와의 관계
Do you have a good **relationship with** your relatives? 너는 네 친척들과 사이가 좋니?

2. 「형용사 + 전치사」

● kind/ mean/ polite/ friendly/ good to somebody ~에게 친절한/ 못된/ 정중한/ 친근한/ 잘 해주는
Be **kind to** everybody. 모두에게 친절해라.

● mad/ upset/ angry about something ~에 대해서 화난
Susie is **mad about** what you said to her. Susie는 네가 그녀에게 한 말에 대해 화가 나있어.

● mad at somebody ~에게 화난
Are you **mad at** me? 나한테 화났니?

● angry at/ with somebody ~에게 화난
I'm not **angry at(with)** you. 나는 너에게 화나지 않았어.

● worried/ nervous/ excited about something ~에 대해 걱정하는/ 긴장한/ 신나는
I'm **worried about** his health. 그의 건강이 걱정이다.
What are you so **nervous about**? 왜 그렇게 긴장하고 있니?

● engaged/ married to somebody ~와 약혼/ 결혼하다

Liz got **married to** a Japanese. Liz는 일본인과 결혼했다.

- tired/ sick of somebody/ something ~에 싫증을 느끼다
  I'm **sick of** eating the same food. 나는 같은 음식 먹는 것에 질렸다.

  - proud/ ashamed/ jealous of somebody/ something ~를 자랑으로 여기는/ 부끄러운/ 질투하는
    I'm **ashamed of** what I did at the party. 파티에서 내가 한 일에 대해 부끄럽다.

3. 「동사 + 전치사」

- apply for a job/ something ~에 지원하다, ~를 신청하다
  Are you going to **apply for** the open position in Sales? 그 영업부 자리에 지원할 거예요?

- belong to somebody ~에게 속하다
  Does this blue coat **belong to** you? 이 파란 코트는 네 것이니?

- care about somebody/ something ~를 상관하다/ 관심 갖다
  She has never **cared about** her appearance. 그녀는 외모에 전혀 신경 쓰지 않아왔다.

- care for somebody/ something ~를 좋아하다, ~를 돌보다
  I don't **care for** coffee that much. 난 커피를 그리 좋아하지 않아요.

- complain about somebody/ something ~에 대해 불평하다
  She **complained about** the high cost of visiting Europe. 그녀는 유럽을 방문하는 데 드는 비싼 비용에 대해 불평했다.

- complain of pain or illness ~를 불평하다
  He **complained of** a headache. 그는 두통을 불평했다.

- consist of something ~로 이루어져 있다
  This book **consists of** 14 chapters. 이 책은 14장으로 이루어져 있다.

- count on somebody/ something ~를 믿다
  There are few people to **count on** around me. 내 주위에는 믿을만한 사람이 거의 없다.

- depend on(upon) somebody/ something ~에 달려있다
  How much it costs **depends upon** how much you buy. 비용이 얼마냐는 네가 얼마나 사느냐에 달려있다.

- dream about somebody/ something ~에 대한 꿈을 꾸다
  What did you **dream about** last night. 어젯밤 무슨 꿈 꿨니?

- dream of somebody/ something ~을 꿈꾸다/ 그리다
  I've **dreamed of** someone like you. 나는 당신 같은 사람을 꿈꿔 왔어요.

- hear about somebody/ something ~에 대해서 듣다
  Did you **hear about** what happened last night? 어젯밤 무슨 일이 있었는지 들었니?

- hear of somebody/ something ~(의 존재)에 대해서 들어보다
  I've never **heard of** the restaurant. Where is it? 나는 그 음식점에 대해 들어본 적이 없어. 어디 있니?

Unit Test

1. 빈칸에 가장 알맞은 전치사를 보기에서 골라 써 넣으시오.

> 보기 | to   about   of   between   for

1. The plane was late, but nobody knew the reason _____ the delay.
2. There are some differences _____ British and American English.
3. What was the cause _____ the accident?
4. Mary is still angry _____ what you said to her.
5. I don't like my job any more. I'm sick _____ it.
6. Thank you. You've been very kind _____ us.
7. I'm really worried _____ your health.
8. Susie is engaged _____ a Canadian.
9. Does this muffler belong _____ you?
10. Would you care _____ a cup of tea?
11. I dreamed _____ you last night.
12. I don't know who Mary Hart is. I've never heard _____ her.

2. 우리말과 일치하도록 괄호 안의 단어를 알맞게 배열하시오.

1. 너는 네 부모님과 사이가 좋니? (a good relationship/ do you have/ with your relatives/ ?)

_____

2. 모두에게 친절해라. (be/ everybody/ kind to)

_____

3. 그녀는 네가 한 일에 대해 화가 나있어. (mad about/ she is/ what you did)

_____

4. 그들은 무엇 때문에 신났니? (they/ what are/ excited about/ ?)

_____

5. 가격은 수요와 공급에 의존한다. (supply and demand/ depend upon/ prices)

_____

6. 너는 네 자신을 부끄러워 해야 돼. (ashamed of/ should be/ yourself/ you)

_____

7. 그 일에 지원해 보지 그러니? (apply for/ the job/ why don't you/ ?)

_____

8. 나는 내 아들이 자랑스럽다. (my son/ proud of/ I'm)

_____

Writing Pattern Practice │ 전치사의 활용

Pattern 1_ 「명사 + 전치사」

그 사고의 원인은 뭐였니?(the cause) _____

너와 나 사이에는 차이점이 좀 있다.(differences) _____

너는 네 부모님과 사이가 좋니?(have a good relationship)

_____

Pattern 2_ 「형용사 + 전치사」

모두에게 친절해라. _____

너는 나에게 화났니?(mad) _____

Mary는 네가 그녀에게 한 말에 대해 화났다.(angry) _____

나는 그의 건강이 걱정이다. _____

너는 왜 그렇게 긴장하고 있니?(What~, so) _____

나는 같은 음식 먹는 것에 질렸다.(sick) _____

나는 네가 자랑스럽다. _____

그녀는 백만장자와 결혼했다.(a millionaire) _____

Pattern 3_ 「동사 + 전치사」

나는 그 일에 지원할 거야. _____

커피 한 잔 드실래요?(Would you like~) _____

그는 두통을 불평했다. _____

가격은 수요와 공급에 의존한다.(supply and demand) _____

나는 어젯밤 네 꿈을 꿨다. _____

나는 가끔 부자가 되는 꿈을 꾼다.(sometimes, be rich)

_____

너는 어제 밤 식당에서 있었던 싸움에 대해서 들었니?(in the restaurant)

_____

Unit

56_ 동사구

● **Pattern** 동사＋전치사
동사＋부사

(At the shopping mall)

A: It is too tight for me, doesn't it?

B: Well, you can get a bigger one. Here you are. You can take it off and try this on.

A: This one fits. How much is it?

B: It's $25.

---

1. 동사구(phrasal verbs)

동사구는 「동사 + in, out, up, down, away, around, about, over, by, out, off, back, through, along 등」의 형태이다.

2. 동사구 + 목적어

목적어가 있는 동사구(동사＋부사)일 경우, 동사구와 목적어의 어순이 중요하다. 목적어가 명사일 때 동사구 사이에 오거나 동사구 뒤에 위치할 수 있지만 대명사일 때 동사구 사이에 와야 한다.

목적어가 명사일 경우: I **put on** my pants. (O) I **put** my pants **on**. (O)

목적어가 대명사일 경우: I **put** them **on**. (O) I **put on** them. (X)

3. 흔히 쓰는 동사구

동사구	예문	동사구	예문
put on 입다, 걸치다	I **put on** my hat. 나는 모자를 썼다. You should **put on** a sweater. 스웨터를 입는게 좋을거야.	take off 벗다, 떼다, 뜨다	**Take off** your coat. 코트를 벗어라 I can't **take** my eyes **off** you. 나는 당신에게서 눈을 뗄 수 없다. The plane is **taking off**. 비행기가 이륙하고 있다.
wake up 깨다, 깨우다	It's time to **wake up**. 일어날 시간이야. **Wake** him **up**. 그를 깨워라.	get up 일어나다	I **get up** at 7. 나는 7시에 일어난다.

동사구	예문	동사구	예문
come in 들어오다	He **came in** the room. 그 는 방에 들어왔다.	come out 나오다, 빠지다	The sun **came out**. 해가 나 왔다. This stain won't **come out**. 이 얼룩이 빠지지 않는다.
go in 들어가다	He **went in** the meeting room. 그는 회의장에 들어갔다.	go out 나가다	The lights **went out**. 전기 가 나갔다.
get in 타다	He **got in** the car. 그는 차 에 탔다.	get out 내리다	**Get out** of the car. 차에서 내려.
get on (올라)타다	I **got on** the elevator. 나 는 엘리베이터에 올랐다.	get off 내리다	They **got off** the bus. 그들 은 버스에서 내렸다.
pick up 데리러 가(오)다, 사다	**Pick** me **up** at 6. 6시에 나 를 데리러와. **Pick up** some milk on your way home. 집에 오는 길에 우유 좀 사와.	drop off 내려주다, 맡기다	**Drop** me **off** over there. 나를 저쪽에서 내려줘. **Drop** it **off** at the front desk 안내 데스크에 맡겨주세요.
turn on (전기나 가스 등을) 켜다	Could you **turn** that TV **on**? TV를 켜 주시겠어요?	turn off (전기나 가스 등을) 끄다	Just **turn** it **off**. 그냥 꺼.
turn up (볼륨 등을) 올리다	I'll **turn up** the volume. (=I'll **turn up** the TV/ radio 등) 볼륨을 올릴게요.	turn down (볼륨 등을) 내리다	I'll **turn down** the volume. (=I'll **turn down** the TV/ radio 등) 볼륨을 내릴게요.
make up 화장하다	**Make up** your face. 화장해.	look out/ (=watch out) 조심하다	**Look out** for cars! 차 조심해! **Watch out!** There is a truck coming. 조심해! 트럭이 오고 있어.
show up 나타나다	He didn't **show up** at the meeting. 그는 회의에 나타나지 않았다.	see off 배웅하다	I'm going to the airport to **see off** my friend. 친구를 배웅하기 위해 공항에 간다.
fill out (양식에) 기입하다	Could you **fill out** this form? 이 양식을 작성해 주실래 요?	throw away 버리다	**Throw** it **away**. 그것을 버려.
put out (담배나 불을) 끄다	Please **put out** your cigarette. 담배를 꺼주세요.	break out 일어나다, 발생하다	A fire **broke out**. 화재가 발 생했다.
put off 연기하다	The wedding has been **put off**. 결혼식이 연기되었다.	come off 떨어져 나오다	The button **came off**. 단추 가 떨어졌다.

Unit Test

1. 빈칸에 문맥상 가장 알맞은 동사구를 보기에서 골라 써 넣으시오.

> 보기 | pick up   look out   put out   show up   wake up

1. I arranged to meet Roy this morning, but he didn't _____.
2. Please _____ your cigarette. You're not allowed to smoke here.
3. _____ for cars!
4. It's already 8 o'clock. _____ your dad.
5. "Give me a ride to the airport." "OK. I'll _____ you _____ at 7.

2. 빈칸에 알맞은 동사구를 써 넣으시오.

1. 그것을 입어라. _____ it _____.
2. 그것을 벗어라. _____ it _____.
3. 네 모자를 써라. _____ your hat.
4. 전기가 나갔다. The lights _____ .
5. 우리는 차에서 내렸다. We _____ the car.
6. 버스가 만원이었다. 우리는 탈 수 없었다. The bus was full. We couldn't _____ .
7. 나는 엘리베이터에서 내렸다. I _____ the elevator.
8. 내가 너를 깨웠니?(=나 때문에 깼니?) Did I _____ you _____ ?
9. 이 양식을 작성해 줄래요? Could you _____ this form?
10. 내가 너를 6시에 데리러 갈게. I'll _____ you _____ at 6.
11. 어떤 여자가 차에 타더니 떠났다. A woman _____ the car and drove off.

3. 우리말과 일치하도록 괄호 안의 단어를 알맞게 배열하시오.

1. 새로운 모델이 나왔다. (came/ a new model/ out)

_____

2. 얼룩이 빠지지 않는다. (won't/ the stain/ come out)

_____

3. 해가 떴다. (up/ came/ the sun)

_____

4. 너 나를 왜 안 깨웠니? (didn't you/ why/ wake me up/ ?)

_____

5. 나를 모퉁이에 내려줘. (me/ at the corner/ drop/ off)

_____

Writing Pattern Practice | 동사구

네 안경을 써. _____

네 양말을 벗어. _____

비행기가 이륙하고 있다. _____

그가 방에 들어왔다. _____

저 영화에는 Brad Pitt이 나왔다. _____

우리는 저녁식사 하러 나갔다. _____

택시에 타라. _____

그녀는 차에서 내렸다. _____

나는 버스를 탔다. _____

우리는 기차에서 내렸다. _____

네 여동생을 깨워라. _____

조심해! There is a car coming. _____

나는 친구를 배웅할 예정이다. _____

그는 회의에 나타나지 않았다. _____

담배를 꺼주세요.(please) _____

나는 그를 데리러 갈거야.(I'll~) _____

나를 저쪽에서 내려줘요.(drop off) _____

회의가 연기되었다.(put off, 현재완료시제) _____

단추가 떨어졌다.(come off) _____

그것들을 버려. _____

남북전쟁이 1861년에 발생했다.(The Civil War) _____

Unit

57 등위접속사/ 상관접속사

● **Pattern**　A and B, A but B, A or B

both A and B, either A or B, neither A nor B

A: **How do you feel about going to a movie tonight?**

B: **Do you have any *particular movie in mind?**

A: **Not really. Let's just go there and see what's on.**

B: **Sure. I'll pick you up at 8.**

*particular 특별한

등위 접속사 and, but, or, so는 문법적 역할이 대등한 「단어」와 「단어」, 「구」와 「구」, 「절」과 「절」을 연결해 주는 역할을 한다.

1. and

● 「A and B」 'A와 B'

I usually have a sandwich **and** milk for breakfast. 나는 보통 아침식사로 샌드위치와 우유를 먹는다.

● 「명령문 + and」 '~해라, 그러면'

Try to do your best, **and** everything will be all right. 최선을 다하도록 해라 그러면 모든 것이 잘 될 것이다.

● to(~하러)의 의미와 같이 쓰이는 and

Go **and** see what he's doing. (=Go to see what he's doing.)

Come **and** see me. (=Come to see me.)

● 「both A and B」 'A와 B 모두'

Both Tom **and** Jane are from the United States. Tom과 Jane은 미국 출신이다.

Mandy is **both** pretty **and** clever. Mandy는 예쁘고 똑똑하다.

2. but

● 「A but B」 'A 그러나 B'

I arrived very early, **but** David arrived even earlier. 나는 매우 일찍 도착했는데 David은 더 일찍 도착했다.

● 「not A but B」 'A가 아니라 B'

Not Cindy **but** you should be responsible for this. Cindy가 아니라 네가 이것에 책임을 져야 한다.

● 「not only A but (also) B」=B as well as A 'A뿐만 아니라 B 역시'

Not only Cindy **but (also)** you should be responsible for this. Cindy 뿐만 아니라 너도 이것에 책임을 져야 한다.

3. or

- 「A or B」 'A 또는 B'
  Would you like coffee **or** tea? 커피 마실래, 차 마실래?
- 「명령문 + or」 '~해라, 그렇지 않으면'
  Come on time, **or** you'll be in trouble. 정각에 와, 그렇지 않으면 곤란해 질 거야.
- 「either A or B」 'A와 B 둘 중 하나'
  Either Sarah **or** I am going to attend the meeting. Sarah나 내가 회의에 참석할 예정이다.
- 「neither A nor B」 'A와 B 둘 다 아닌'
  Neither Sam **nor** Amy was there. Sam과 Amy 모두 거기에 없었다.

> **I MORE TIPS I** 다음의 접속사들이 나오는 경우 동사의 수는 내용상 중요한 명사, 또는 동사와 위치가 가까운 명사에 수를 일치시킨다.
> both A and B : 'A와 B 둘 다'의 의미로 복수동사 사용
> not only A but also B (= B as well as A) : B에 일치
> not A but B : B에 일치
> either A or B : B에 일치
> neither A nor B : B에 일치

4. so

so는 결과를 나타내는 접속사로 so 다음에 결과의 내용이 온다.
I didn't have a watch, **so** I didn't know the time. 시계가 없어서 시간을 몰랐다.
I left my key inside, **so** I'm locked out of the room. 열쇠를 안에 놔둬서 방문이 잠겨서 못 들어 간다.

> **I MORE TIPS I** 등위접속사 and, but, or, so는 같은 종류의 말을 연결시키는 병렬구조를 가진다. 즉, 등위접속사에 의해 앞뒤로 연결된 말은 서로 품사가 같거나 구조가 같아야 한다. (Unit 58 참조)
>
> I like <u>apples</u> and <u>pears</u>. 〔명사 and 명사〕
> He's a <u>handsome</u> but <u>boring</u> person. 〔형용사 but 형용사〕
> <u>To be</u> or <u>not to be</u>; that is the question. 〔to부정사 or to부정사〕
> She might be <u>in her office</u> or <u>at the meeting</u>. 〔전치사구 or 전치사구〕
> <u>She's from Canada</u> and <u>he's from Australia</u>. 〔절 and 절〕

Unit Test

1. 빈칸에 and, but, or, nor 중 가장 알맞은 접속사를 써 넣으시오.

1. He _____ I are close friends.
2. She's pretty _____ boring.
3. Work out regularly, _____ you'll get thinner.
4. My father neither smokes _____ drinks.
5. "Would you like coffee _____ tea?" "Coffee, please."
6. Either she goes _____ I go.
7. She both dances _____ sings.
8. I can't remember his name exactly. It was Briarly _____ something.
9. I both play the piano _____ the violin.
10. She neither smiled, spoke, _____ looked at me.

2. 빈칸에 알맞은 접속사를 써 넣으시오.

1. (동전의) 앞면 할래, 뒷면 할래?
   Heads _____ tails?
2. 그녀는 예쁘고 똑똑하다.
   She's both pretty _____ clever.
3. 우리는 마시고 이야기하고 춤췄다.
   We drank, talked, _____ danced.
4. 그 장소는 추울 뿐 아니라 습했다.
   The place was not only cold, _____ also damp.
5. 너는 지금 나와 집에 가거나 걸어가.
   You can either come with me now _____ walk home.
6. 늦어서 서둘렀다.
   I was late, _____ I hurried up.

3. 우리말과 일치하도록 괄호 안의 단어를 알맞게 배열하시오.

1. Mary는 중국어를 말하고 쓴다. (both/ speaks and/ Mary/ writes Chinese)

_____

2. 그는 시카고 또는 뉴욕에 있다. (or/ Chicago/ he's in/ New York/ either)

_____

3. Sally는 예쁠 뿐만 아니라 똑똑하다. (but also/ pretty/ Sally is/ clever/ not only)

_____

Writing Pattern Practice | 등위접속사/ 상관접속사

Pattern 1_ 「A and B」, 「명령문 + and」, 「동사 + and(to= ~하러) + 동사」, 「both A and B」

나는 야채와 우유를 샀다. _____

가서 그가 무엇을 하고 있는지 봐.(=Go to see what he's doing.)

나를 보러 와.(=Come to see me.) _____

Tom과 Jane은 둘 다 미국 출신이다.(Both~) _____

Jack은 차와 오토바이 둘 다 고친다.(repair, motobikes)

_____

Pattern 2_ 「A but B」, 「not A but B」, 「not only A but (also) B」

그는 잘생겼지만 지루하다. _____

Cindy가 아니라 네가 와야 한다.(should) _____

Cindy 뿐만 아니라 너도 와야 한다. _____

Pattern 3_ 「A or B」, 「명령문, or」, 「either A or B」, 「neither A nor B」

커피 마실래, 차 마실래?(Would you like~) _____

지금 일어나, 그렇지 않으면 버스 놓칠 거야. _____

Sarah나 내가 회의에 참석할 예정이다.(Either~) _____

그것은 흥미롭지도 않고 사실도 아니다.(That's~, true)_____

너는 맞지도 틀리지도 않다.(right) _____

Pattern 4_ 「절 + so + (결과)절」

그는 늦어서 서둘렀다. _____

나는 시계가 없어서 시간을 몰랐다. _____

Unit
58_ 문장의 병렬구조

● Pattern	단어＋접속사＋단어
	구＋접속사＋구
	절＋ 접속사＋절

A: Monica! I was just having dinner. Do you want some of this?

B: No, I'm fine. Are you eating pizza again? It's not good for your health.

A: Sometimes I cook nice meals for myself.

B: Stop eating junk food and try to eat healthy food.

1. 문장의 병렬구조

접속사는 문법적 기능이 동일할 경우 형태가 같은 단어와 구, 절을 연결한다. 항상 병렬구조를 취하는 접속사는 and, but, or, not only～ but also…, not～ but…, both～ and…, either～ or…, neither～ nor… 등이다.

● 단어 + 접속사 + 단어

He was <u>poor</u> **but** <u>honest.</u> 그는 가난하지만 정직했다.
　　　　형용사　　　　형용사
I like **both** <u>reading</u> **and** <u>sleeping.</u> 나는 독서와 잠자는 것을 좋아한다.
　　　　　동명사　　　　　　동명사

● 구 + 접속사 + 구

People swim **not only** <u>in summer</u> **but also** <u>in winter.</u> 사람들은 여름뿐만 아니라 겨
　　　　　　　　　　전치사구　　　　　　　　전치사구
울에도 수영한다.

● 절 + 접속사 + 절

<u>We brought the food</u> **and** <u>they supplied the drink.</u> 우리는 음식을 가져왔고 그들은 음
　　　　　　문장　　　　　　　　　　　　　　문장
료수를 제공했다.

2. 반복을 피하기 위한 생략

불필요한 반복을 피하기 위해 접속사를 중심으로 앞에 언급되었던 단어들은 생략할 수 있음을 유의한다.

I have taught English **in Seoul, (in) Busan,** and **(in) Daegu.** 나는 서울에서, 부산
(에서) 그리고 대구(에서) 영어를 가르쳐왔다.

Charlie **not only** <u>bought a new car</u> **but also** <u>(bought) a new motorbike.</u>
Charlie는 새 차 뿐만 아니라 새 오토바이도 (샀다).

Unit Test

1. 보기와 같이 '접속사 + 병렬구조'에 밑줄 치시오.

> 보기 | I play <u>both tennis and badminton.</u>

    1. They drank and danced.
    2. Either Mary or I will go there.
    3. Benny likes golf but hates tennis.
    4. He had a bad temper, but everybody liked him.
    5. I neither like nor dislike him.
    6. The man is sleeping and snoring.
    7. Would you like coffee or tea?
    8. Neither Kate nor Sue was there.
    9. He neither smokes nor drinks.
   10. Erin not only plays the piano, but also the violin.

2. 보기와 같이 주어진 접속사를 이용하여 두 문장을 병렬구조의 한 문장으로 연결하시오. 단, 반복되는 불필요한 단어는 생략한다.

> 보기 | Ann was late. Tom was late. (both~ and···)
>   → <u>Both Ann and Tom was late.</u>

1. I was hungry. I was tired.(and)
→ _____

2. I ate breakfast. I didn't eat lunch.(but)
→ _____

3. David was tired of studying English. Nick was tired of studying English.(both~ and···)
→ _____

4. He is American. He is Canadian.(either~or···)
→ _____

5. Jenny can't come to the party. Ann can't come to the party.(neither~ nor···)
→ _____

Writing Pattern Practice | 문장의 병렬구조

Pattern 1_ 단어 + 접속사 + 단어

나는 셔츠와 바지를 샀다. _____

나는 독서와 잠자는 것을 좋아한다. _____

그는 천천히 하지만 분명하게 말했다.(talk) _____

커피를 드실래요, 차를 드실래요?(Would you like~) _____

_____

Mary 또는 내가 거기에 갈 거야.(Either~, or) _____

나는 그를 좋아하지도 않고 싫어하지도 않는다.(neither~ nor, dislike) _____

_____

Pattern 2_ 구 + 접속사 + 구

나는 스키와 스케이트 타는 것을 좋아한다.(to ski, to skate) _____

_____

사람들은 여름뿐만 아니라 겨울에도 수영한다.(in summer) _____

_____

Pattern 3_ 절 + 접속사 + 절

우리는 음식을 가져왔고 그들은 음료수를 제공했다.(supply the drink) _____

_____

두 소년은 외모에서 닮았지만 성격에서 다르다.(alike in looks, in personality) _____

_____

Pattern 4_ 반복을 피하기 위한 생략

나는 서울에서, 부산(에서) 그리고 대구(에서) 영어를 가르쳐왔다. _____

_____

Charlie는 새 차를 샀을 뿐만 아니라 새 오토바이도 (샀다).(not only~, but also) _____

_____

Erin은 피아노를 칠 뿐만 아니라 바이올린도 (켠다). _____

1. 빈칸에 알맞은 전치사를 써 넣고, 전치사가 필요 없으면 X표 하시오.

1. 월요일 아침에 만나.
   See you _____ Monday morning.

2. 그녀는 스위스에서 자랐다.
   She grew up _____ Switzerland.

3. 그는 공항에 15:00시에 도착한다.
   He arrives _____ the airport at 15:00.

4. 나는 학교에 자전거 타고 갈 거야.
   I'll go to school _____ my bike.

5. 차에서 내려.
   Get _____ the car.

6. 오늘 아침 시간 있니?
   Are you free _____ this afternoon?

7. 아무 때나 와.
   Come _____ any time.

8. 나는 12월에 태어났다.
   I was born _____ December.

9. 강 위에 있는 다리를 봐.
   Look at the bridge _____ the river.

10. 그는 하루 종일 잤다.
    He slept _____ all day.

11. 크리스마스 날에 우리를 보러와.
    Come and see us _____ Christmas Day.

12. 너는 수요일에 뭐하니?
    What are you doing _____ Wednesday?

13. 해가 졌다.
    The sun went _____ .

14. Susan은 문 옆에 있었다.
    Susan was _____ the door.

15. 나는 저녁마다 집에 있다.
    I'm at home _____ every evening.

16. 나는 아침에 일이 잘된다.
    I work best _____ the morning.

17. 우리는 터널을 통과했다.
    We passed _____ a tunnel.

18. 너는 늦어도 6시까지 그것을 돌려줘야 해.
    You must bring it back _____ six at the latest.

19. 아기는 엄마가 올 때까지 계속 울었다.
    The baby went on crying _____ her mother came.

20. Las Vegas에 가는 가장 쉬운 방법은 무엇인가요?
    What's the easiest way to get _____ Las Vegas?

1. 빈칸에 들어갈 알맞은 전치사를 보기에서 골라 써 넣으시오.

보기 | about   at   of   for   between   with   to

1. Are you still mad _____ me?
2. What are you so nervous _____ ?
3. There are some differences _____ British and American English.
4. There is a reason _____ every important thing that happens.
5. I have a good relationship _____ my boss.
6. I'm proud _____ what you did yesterday.
7. Does this bag belong _____ you?

2. 틀린 곳을 찾아 밑줄치고 고쳐 쓰시오. 틀린 곳이 없으면 O표 하시오.

1. I put my hat on.　　　　　　　　　　　　　→ _____
2. Pick up me at 8.　　　　　　　　　　　　　→ _____
3. Please put your cigarette out.　　　　　　　→ _____
4. Why are you wearing your coat in here? Take it off. → _____
5. Drop off me in front of the post office.　　　→ _____
6. Both Janet and I were at the meeting.　　　→ _____
7. Not only Tom but also you are invited to the party. → _____
8. Either Sarah nor I am going to attend the meeting. → _____
9. Neither Sam or Cindy is from the United states. → _____
10. Would you like coffee but tea?　　　　　　→ _____

※ 빈칸에 들어갈 알맞은 말은?

3. "When did it happen?" "_____ the summer"

① for　　② during　　③ at　　④ on

4. "How long has it rained?" "It has rained _____ a week."

① for　　② during　　③ at　　④ on

5. It's been a long time _____ I saw you.

① for　　② since　　③ in　　④ about

6. Either you'll leave this house_____I'll call the police.

① and　　② but　　③ or　　④ so

7. 다음 글을 읽고, 문맥상 빈칸에 들어갈 알맞은 전치사를 고르시오.

Do you have a garden in your house? In some communities in Korea, people have gardens. One side of garden may be planted with vegetables. The other side may be planted with flowers and trees.

People are getting more interested in their health now. The vegetables we grow are good to eat. It helps us grow and get the nutrients we need to stay healthy. Some vegetables grow _____ the ground, and some grow underground.

The flower gardens are very beautiful. When the flowers bloom, you can cut them and make beautiful flower arrangements for your house.

① above   ② through   ③ in   ④ off

※다음 글을 읽고, 질문에 답하시오. (8-9)

You might have seen Hello Kitty many times. Hello Kitty is the most famous cartoon cat. Sanrio Company made her popular everywhere in the world. She is really pretty, has a little nose and usually wears a bow or a flower on her head. There are over 22,000 kinds of products that have pictures of Kitty on them, such as bags, clothes and pens. They have been sold in about 40 countries.

Not only children____ⓐ____also adults are buying Hello Kitty products. Sanrio's biggest success is its

ability to create products that appeal to women in their 20s and 30s around the world. Why do you guess people like Hello Kitty? Perhaps it is because she doesn't have a mouth, ____ⓑ____she does not look happy or sad. When people feel happy, they can look at her and think she is happy too. When they are depressed, they think she is depressed too. People feel she is a friend who feels the same as they do.

8. ⓐ에 들어갈 알맞은 말을 고르시오.

① and   ② but   ③ or   ④ so

9. ⓑ에 들어갈 가장 알맞은 말을 고르시오.

① and   ② but   ③ or   ④ so

* Chapter 7 | 복잡한 문장구조 이해하기

59 that, whether, if로 시작하는 명사절

● Pattern that, whether, if＋주어＋동사

A: You look pale. Are you OK?
B: Not really. I'm feeling under the weather today and I'm a little dizzy.
A: I hope (that) it's nothing serious.
B: I think (that) it's because of the weather. It's hot and humid.

1. **명사절을 만드는 that '~라는 것'**

접속사 that과 연결된 절은 명사절을 만들 수 있다. 즉 문장 안에서 주어, 목적어, 보어 자리에 사용된다.

● 주어 역할
  That he knows everything is obvious. 그가 모든 것을 알고 있다는 것은 명백하다.
  = <u>It</u> is obvious **that he knows everything.** (가주어 it 사용)
  = <u>The fact</u> **that** he knows everything is obvious. (The fact that ~ 사용)
  *that절이 주어역할을 할 경우 주로 가주어 it이나 The fact that~을 이용해 표현한다.

● 목적어 역할 (*이 때 that은 생략가능)
  I hope **(that) you'll have a wonderful time.** 네가 좋은 시간 보내기를 바란다.

● 보어 역할
  The problem is **that your English is not so good.** 문제는 네 영어가 서툰 것이다.

2. **명사절을 만드는 whether, if '~인지 아닌지'**

if와 whether는 의문문을 명사절로 만들어 간접의문문에서 사용할 수 있는 접속사들이다.

1. whether (~or not)

● 주어 역할
  Whether he's rich (or not) isn't important. 그가 부자인지 아닌지는 중요하지 않다.

● 목적어 역할
  Do you know **whether the rumor is true (or not)?** 그 소문이 사실인지 아닌지 아니?

● 보어 역할
  The question is **whether the man can be trusted (or not).** 문제는 그 남자가 믿을만한지 아닌지 이다.

2. if

if는 주로 목적어 자리에 사용된다.

● 목적어역할
  I'm not sure **if I'll have time.** 내가 시간이 있을지 모르겠다.

Unit Test

1. 다음은 명사절 앞에 that이 빠진 문장들이다. that이 들어갈 곳에 ✓표 하시오.

1. I heard you'd got a new job.
2. I believe this is your coat.
3. It's obvious he doesn't have enough money to buy that car.
4. The fact is she came here for money.
5. Tell me you love me.
6. The problem is she doesn't speak English well.
7. It is a fact smoking can cause cancer.
8. The point is you're skinny enough now.
9. I thought you'd get lost.
10. You knew I wouldn't forget your birthday.

2. 다음 의문문을 whether(if)을 사용한 명사절로 바꾸어 문장을 완성하시오. 보기를 참고하시오.

> 보기 | Does he go to school?
>   → I'd like to know <u>whether(if) he goes to school</u>.

1. Is she single?
→ I'd like to know _____.
2. Is there an ATM near here?
→ I'd like to know _____.
3. Does he have a lot of money?
→ I'd like to know _____.
4. Does Jane love me?
→ I'd like to know _____.
5. Are you coming to my birthday party?
→ Tell me _____.
6. Should I move to a new house?
→ Tell me _____.
7. Can you lend me some money?
→ Tell me _____.
8. Can you help me with my homework?
→ Tell me _____.

Writing Pattern Practice | that, whether, if로 시작하는 명사절

Pattern 1_ 「that + 주어 + 동사」 '~라는 것'

그가 여전히 미혼이라는 것은 놀라운 일이다.(It's surprising~, single)

_____

네가 결혼했다는 것은 모두에게 알려져 있다.(It is known to everybody~)

_____

네가 좋은 시간 보내기를 바란다.(hope, wonderful) _____

나는 그것이 좋은 생각이라고 생각한다. _____

문제는 네 영어가 서툰 것이다.(The problem is~) _____

요점은 돈이 전부가 아니라는 것이다.(The point~) _____

중요한 것은 네가 행복한 것이다. _____

Pattern 2_ 「whether + 주어 + 동사」 '~인지 아닌지'

그가 부자인지 아닌지는 중요하지 않다. _____

너는 그 소문이 사실인지 아닌지 아니?(the rumor)_____

문제는 그 남자가 믿을만한지 아닌지이다.(The question is~, trust)

_____

우리는 우리가 머물러야 할 지 떠나야 할 지 결정 못하겠다.(should, leave)

_____

Pattern 3_ 「if + 주어 + 동사」 '~인지 아닌지'

내가 시간이 있을지 모르겠다.(I'm not sure~) _____

나는 그가 경기에서 이길지 궁금하다.(I wonder~) _____

나는 내일 비가 올지 모른다. _____

나는 그녀가 내게 돈을 빌려줄 수 있는지 물었다.(ask, could)

_____

Unit

60 의문사로 시작하는 명사절

● Pattern

| 의문사(+주어) + 동사 + 동사~ [주어역할] |
| 주어 + 동사 + 의문사(+주어) + 동사 [목적어역할] |
| 주어+be/ 2형식동사+의문사(+주어) +동사 [보어역할] |

A: Wow. Your Japanese is quite good.

B: Thank you.

A: Tell me who taught you Japanese.

B: Actually, I used to live in Japan for a couple of years.

의문문이 다른 문장 속에서 명사절로 쓰여 주어, 목적어, 보어 역할을 하는 것을 간접의문이라고 한다. 이때 의문문의 본래 어순인 「의문사 + 동사 + 주어」는 간접의문문에서는 「의문사 + 주어 + 동사」 형태로 바뀐다는 점에 유의한다.

1. 의문문 : 「의문사 + 동사 + 주어」 → 명사절 : 「의문사 + 주어 + 동사」

주어 + is the question + who(m) does she love? _{의문문}	→ **Who(m) she loves** is the question. _{명사절(주어역할)} 그녀가 누구를 사랑하는지 의문이다.
I don't know + 목적어 + what did he do last night? _{의문문}	→ I don't know **what he did last night**. _{명사절(목적어역할)} 나는 그가 어젯밤 무엇을 했는지 모른다.
The question is + 보어 + Where is she from? _{의문문}	→ The question is **where she is from**. _{명사절(보어역할)} 그녀가 어디 출신인지 의문이다.

I MORE TIPS I 의문사 자신이 주어일 경우에는 명사절에서 그대로 「의문사 + 동사」 형태로 쓴다.
Tell me. + Who taught you English?
→ Tell me **who taught you English**. 누가 네게 영어를 가르쳐 줬는지 말해라.

2. 「의문사 + do you think, believe, guess, suppose, imagine + 주어 + 동사~ ?」

의문사로 시작하는 명사절이 think, believe, guess, suppose, imagine 동사의 목적어 역할을 하는 경우 의문사가 맨 앞으로 온다.

| Do you think + 목적어?
+
when does the movie start? | → **When** do you think **the movie starts?**
영화가 언제 시작하는 것 같니? |
| Do you guess + 목적어?
+
where is she? | → **Where** do you guess **she is?**
그녀가 어디에 있는 것 같니? |

Unit Test

1. 두 문장을 하나로 연결하여 쓰시오.

1. Do you know + Why didn't she come?

_____

2. Do you guess? + When did it happen?

_____

3. I don't know + What is her phone number?

_____

4. Do you suppose? + Where is Tom?

_____

5. I know + Where does she live?

_____

6. Tell me + Who can help me.

_____

7. Do you think? + Who is he?

_____

8. I asked him + How did he go to the mall?

_____

9. I wonder + How old she is?

_____

10. Do you imagine? + Who stole the money?

_____

2. 우리말과 일치하도록 괄호 안의 단어를 알맞게 배열하시오.

1. 그녀를 누가 대신할 것 같니? (do you suppose/ who/ will/ replace her/ ?)

_____

2. 그가 무슨 일을 하는 것 같니? (he does/ what/ do you think/ ?)

_____

3. 무엇이 답인 것 같니? (what/ is/ the answer/ do you believe/ ?)

_____

4. 내가 다음에 무엇을 할 것 같니? (do you guess/ I will do next/ what/ ?)

_____

5. Tom이 어디에 있는 것 같니? (where/ Tom is/ do you think/ ?)

_____

Writing Pattern Practice │ 의문사로 시작하는 명사절

Pattern 1_ 「**의문사 + 주어 + 동사 + 동사~** 」
　　　　　　　명사절(주어역할)
　　　　「**주어 + 동사 + 의문사 + 주어 + 동사**」
　　　　　　　　　　　명사절(목적어역할)
　　　「**주어 + be동사/ 2형식동사 + 의문사 + 주어 + 동사**」
　　　　　　　　　　　　　　명사절(보어역할)

그녀가 누구를 사랑하는지 의문이다.(~is the question)

나는 그가 어젯밤 무엇을 했는지 모른다.　_____

의문은 그녀가 어디 출신인가이다.(The questions is~)

_____

나는 그의 이름이 무엇인지 알고 싶다.(want)　_____

그는 그가 누구를 만났는지 나에게 말하지 않았다.(tell)

_____

Pattern 2_ 「**의문사 + 동사 + 동사~** 」 – 의문사가 주어일 경우
　　　　　　　명사절(주어역할)
　　　　「**주어 + 동사 + 의문사 + 동사**」
　　　　　　　　　명사절(목적어역할)
　　　「**주어 + be동사/ 2형식동사 + 의문사 + 동사**」
　　　　　　　　　　　　　명사절(보어역할)

누가 나를 태워 줄 수 있는지 알고 싶다.(give me a ride)

_____

나는 그가 무슨 일로 여기에 왔는 지 모른다.(~what brought him here)

_____

의문은 누가 그 돈을 가져갔는가이다.(take)　_____

Pattern 3_ 「**의문사 + do you think, believe, guess, suppose, imagine + 주어 + 동사~ ?**」

너는 영화가 언제 시작하는 것 같니?(think)　_____

너는 그녀가 어디에 있는 것 같니?(guess)　_____

너는 그 사고가 언제 일어난 것 같니?(suppose, happen)　_____

너는 어떻게 그가 여기에서 빠져나간 것 같니?(suppose, get out of)

_____

Pattern 4_ 「**의문사 + do you think, believe, guess, suppose, imagine + 동사~ ?**」 – 의문사가 주어일 경우

너는 누가 네게 선물을 보낸 것 같니?(think)　_____

너는 무엇이 답인 것 같니?(guess)　_____

Unit

61 형용사절의 쓰임과 종류

● Pattern   선행사+who/whom/which(+주어)+동사

형용사 역할

A: Do you have a seating preference, sir?
B: I'd like an aisle seat which has extra legroom, if possible.
A: Yes, I have a seat next to the emergency exit. Here's your boarding pass.
B: Thanks. I appreciate it.

---

1. 형용사, 형용사구, 형용사절

형용사는 명사를 수식하고 설명한다. 형용사 역할을 하는 것은 형용사, 형용사구, 형용사절 등이 있다.

● 형용사
He's **handsome** and **sweet.** 그는 잘생기고 다정하다.

● 형용사구
Look at the picture **on the wall.** 벽에 있는 그림을 봐라.

● 형용사절
The woman **who lives next door** is friendly. 옆집에 사는 그 여자는 친절하다.

2. 형용사절

명사 뒤에서 앞에 있는 명사(선행사)를 꾸며주는 절을 형용사절이라고 한다. 이때 이런 형용사절을 이끌면서 일종의 접속사 및 대명사 역할을 하는 것을 「관계대명사」라고 한다. 관계대명사에는 who, whom, whose, which 등이 있다.

> This is <u>the key.</u> 이것은 열쇠다. + <u>It</u> opens the garage. 그것은 차고를 연다.
>
> This is <u>the key **which** opens the garage.</u> 이것은 차고를 여는 열쇠다.
>   선행사   형용사절

3. 관계대명사 who, whom, whose

관계대명사 who, whom, whose는 선행사가 사람일 때 쓰며, 선행사가 문장 안에서 주어역할을 하면 who, 목적어역할을 하면 whom, 소유격역할을 하면 whose를 쓴다.

● who : 주어역할
Those are <u>the people</u> **who** live next door. 저 사람들이 옆집에 사는 사람들이다.
(←Those are **the people**. + **They** live next door.)

- whom : 목적어역할 *whom 대신 who를 쓰기도 하는데 목적격 관계대명사는 생략하는 경우도 많다.

  Sally is <u>a person</u> **who(m)** everybody loves. Sally는 모든 사람들이 사랑하는 사람이다.
  (←Sally is **a person**. + Everybody loves **her**.)

- whose : 소유격역할

  I saw <u>a girl</u> **whose** hair is blonde. 나는 머리가 금발인 소녀를 봤다.
  (←I saw **a girl**. + **Her** hair is blonde.)

4. 관계대명사 which

관계대명사 which는 선행사가 사람 이외의 것일 때 쓴다. 주격, 목적격은 which를 쓰고 소유격은 of which 또는 whose를 쓴다.

- which : 주어역할

  This is the house **which** has 9 bedrooms. 침실이 9개인 집이다.

- which : 목적어역할

  There's some bread **which** you might like. 네가 좋아할 것 같은 빵이 있어.

- whose (of which) : 소유격역할

  This is the book **whose** name is *Love*. 이것은 제목이 '사랑'인 책이다.

| MORE TIPS | 소유격 관계대명사 whose, of which는 비교적 딱딱한 표현으로 일상회화에서는 상황에 따라 다른 방법으로 표현하는 경우가 많다.
This is the car **whose** seats are 5. → This is the car with 5 seats. (more natural)
This is the car which has 5 seats. (more natural)

5. 관계대명사 that

- who나 which를 대신하는 that

  관계대명사 that은 관계대명사 who나 which 대신 사용할 수 있다.
  I like people **that(=who)** smile a lot. 나는 많이 웃는 사람들을 좋아한다.

- 선행사에 최상급, 서수, the very, the only, all, every 등이 포함된 경우 that을 사용하는 편이 자연스럽지만, 선행사가 사람일 경우 who를 쓸 수도 있다.

  Is this all **that** is left? 이것이 남은 것 전부니?
  It's the best book **that** I've ever read. 그것은 내가 읽은 것 중 최고의 책이다.
  All **that** I say is true. 내가 말하는 것은 모두 진실이다.
  Who is the first person **who** invented a telephone? 전화를 처음 발명한 사람이 누구지?

| MORE TIPS | 관계대명사의 생략
1. 목적격 관계대명사의 경우 흔히 생략되는 경우가 많다.
   Do you remember the people (who) we met in London? 런던에서 만난 사람들을 기억해?
2. 「주격 관계대명사＋be동사」의 경우 역시 생략할 수 있다.
   The man (who is) wearing sunglasses is my boss. 선글라스를 쓰고 있는 사람이 내 상사이다.

Unit Test

1. 두 문장을 관계대명사를 이용하여 한 문장으로 만드시오.

1. Have you got the book? + The book is really easy to read.

_____

2. The movie was very good. + Michael recommended the movie to me.

_____

3. That's the man. + I really wanted to see the man.

_____

4. I went to see Mr. and Mrs. Hart. + I looked after their children a few years ago.

_____

5. I have a vacuum cleaner. + You can use the vacuum cleaner.

_____

6. Britney Spears is a singer. + She is very famous in the world.

_____

7. I have something. + It will clean that carpet.

_____

8. This is the house. + The house has three bedrooms.

_____

9. Where is that nurse? + I saw her last time.

_____

10. She married a man. + she met the man on a bus.

_____

2. 밑줄친 관계대명사 중 생략할 수 있는 것에만 X표 하시오.

1. The job <u>that</u> he got was very tiring.
2. The professor Lee is a person <u>who</u> I really respect.
3. That's the woman <u>who</u> lives next door.
4. The doctor <u>who</u> treated me wasn't very kind.
5. They never thanked me for the money <u>that</u> I lent them.
6. That's the woman <u>who</u> I'm going to marry.
7. I've lost the ring <u>which</u> Michael gave me.
8. I saw a girl <u>whose</u> beauty took my breath away.
9. Did you like the wine <u>that</u> we drank last night?
10. The woman <u>who</u> does my hair has moved to another hairdresser's.

Writing Pattern Practice | 형용사절의 쓰임과 종류

Pattern 1_ 「선행사 + <u>who, whom, whose~</u>」 선행사가 사람일 때

나는 너를 아는 남자를 만났어.   _____

저 사람들이 옆집에 사는 사람들이다.(Those are~) _____

적게 먹는 사람이 더 오래 산다.(less)   _____

Sally는 모든 사람들이 사랑하는 사람이다.(a person)

  _____

너는 우리가 회의에서 만난 사람들을 기억하니? _____

나는 머리가 금발인 소녀를 봤다.(whose, blonde) _____

Pattern 2_ 「선행사 + <u>which~</u>」 선행사가 사람 이외의 것일 때

너는 내가 사용할 수 있는 펜을 가지고 있니? _____

네가 좋아할 것 같은 빵이 있어.(~you might like) _____

저것은 침실을 세 개 가지고 있는 집이다.(That is~) _____

Pattern 3_ 「선행사 + <u>that~</u>」 who나 which를 대신할 때

나는 많이 웃는 사람들을 좋아한다.(~smile a lot) _____

너는 이 카펫을 깨끗하게 할 무언가를 가지고 있니?(anything, will)

그가 구한 일은 따분했다.(get, boring)   _____

너는 우리가 어제 먹은 스테이크 좋았니?   _____

그것은 내가 읽은 것 중 최고의 책이다.   _____

내가 말하는 것은 모두 진실이다.(All that~) _____

62 관계대명사 what

● **Pattern**   선행사+~~what~~(+주어)+동사
명사역할

 Grammar in Practice

A: Can you see the screen?
B: No. I can't see very well. The man in front of me is too tall.
A: That's what I thought. Why don't we switch seats?
B: You are so *thoughtful. Thanks.

*thoughtful 사려 깊은

 Grammar in Use

1. 선행사를 포함하는 관계대명사 what

관계대명사 what은 선행사를 포함하며 「the thing(s) which/that~」과 바꿔 쓸 수 있다. 따라서 what이 이끄는 절은 '~하는 것'의 의미로 문장에서 명사역할을 한다.

> She showed me **the thing**. She bought **it** yesterday.
> →She showed me **the thing which** she bought yesterday.
> 형용사절
> →She showed me **what** she bought yesterday.
> 명사절

The thing which(=that) she said made me angry.
→**What she said** made me confused. 그녀가 한 말은 나를 혼란스럽게 했다.
주어역할

He can give you **the thing which(=that) you need**.
→He can give you **what you need.** 그는 네가 필요한 것을 줄 수 있다.
목적어역할

This is exactly **the thing which(=that) I wanted**.
→This is exactly **what I wanted.** 이것은 내가 원했던 바로 그것이다.
보어역할

I MORE TIPS I 관계대명사 what은 '~하는 모든 것'이라는 all that의 의미로 쓰이기도 한다.
She lost **what(=all that)** she owned. 그녀는 가진 것을 (모두) 잃었다.

2. 관계대명사 what을 포함한 관용적 표현

● 「what + 주어 + have/has」 ~의 재산
  I'm not interested in **what she has**. 나는 그녀가 가진 것에 관심없다.

● 「what + 주어 + be동사」 ~의 상태, 인격 등
  He is not **what he used to be**. 그는 옛날의 그가 아니다.

● 「what is + 비교급/최상급」 더욱 ~한 것은/ 가장 ~한 것은
  Ted is nice, and **what is better**, he is handsome. Ted는 친절하다, 더 좋은 것은 그는 잘생겼다.

● 「what we/you/they call (=what is called)」 소위 말하자면
  Sam is, **what is called**, a millionaire. Sam은 소위 말해서 백만장자이다.

Unit Test

1. 보기와 같이 두 문장을 관계대명사 what을 사용하여 한 문장으로 만드시오.

> 보기 | This is the thing. + I wanted it.
> → This is what I wanted.

1. I can't believe that. + You said that.

→ _____

2. My sister gave me the thing. + I needed it.

→ _____

3. I didn't agree with that. + You explained that to me.

→ _____

4. This is the thing. + I have it.

→ _____

5. He showed me the thing. + He bought it yesterday.

→ _____

6. She lost the thing. + she owned it.

→ _____

2. 우리말과 일치하도록 괄호 안의 단어를 알맞게 배열하시오.

1. 내가 원하는 것은 앉을 곳이다. (a place to sit down/ I want is/ what)

_____

2. 이것은 Tom이 만든 것이다. (this is/ Tom made/ what)

_____

3. 나는 예전의 내가 아니다. (I used to be/ I'm not /what)

_____

4. 그녀가 한 말은 나를 화나게 만들었다. (made me angry/ what/ she said)

_____

5. 나는 그녀에게 그녀가 필요한 것을 줬다. (what/ I gave her/ she needed)

_____

6. 그가 필요한 것은 돈이다. (he needs/ money/ what/ is)

_____

7. 내가 알고 싶은 것은 그의 전화번호이다. (what/ is his phone number/ I want to know)

_____

Writing Pattern Practice | 관계대명사 what

Pattern 1_ 「선행사 + what (+ 주어) + 동사」

그녀가 말한 것은 나를 화나게 만들었다.(What she said~)

_____

돈은 나를 행복하게 만들어 주는 것이 아니다. _____

그는 내게 내가 필요한 것을 줄 수 있다. _____

이것은 Tom이 만든 것이다. _____

이것은 내가 원했던 것이다. _____

그녀는 가진 것을 잃었다.(own) _____

내가 원하는 것은 앉을 곳이다.(a place) _____

그가 필요한 것은 돈이다. _____

내가 알고 싶은 것은 그의 전화번호이다. _____

나는 네가 무슨 말을 하고 있는지 이해할 수 없다.(understand, talk about)

_____

나는 네가 지난 여름에 한 일을 알고 있다. _____

내가 말하려고 하는 것은 내가 너를 사랑한다는 것이다.(What I'm trying~)

_____

Pattern 2_ 관계대명사 what을 포함한 관용적 표현

- 「what + 주어 + have/has」 ~의 재산
나는 그녀가 가진 것에 관심 없다.(be interested in~)_____

- 「what + 주어 + be동사」 ~의 상태, 인격 등
나는 옛날의 내가 아니다.(used to) _____

- 「what is + 비교급/최상급」 더욱 ~한 것은/ 가장 ~한 것은
Sally는 매력적이다, 그리고 더욱 좋은 것은 그녀는 착하다.(attractive, good-natured)

_____

Nick은 자기 중심적이다, 그리고 더욱 나쁜 것은 그는 멍청하다.(self-centered, dull)

_____

- 「what we/you/they call (=what is called)」 소위 말하자면
Sam은 소위 말해서 백마탄 왕자님이다.(Prince Charming)

_____

Unit
63 관계부사

● **Pattern** 선행사 + <u>where/when/why/(how)</u> + 주어 + 동사

A: I'm frustrated. I'm too fat. I think I should go on a diet.
B: Honey, you don't have to. I like the way you are. You are just perfect.

---

1. 관계부사 where/ when/ why/ how

관계부사는 형용사절을 이끌어 명사를 꾸며준다. 두 문장을 하나로 연결하는 접속사와 부사역할을 동시에 하며, 우리말로 해석하지 않는다. 관계부사는 대부분 that으로 바꾸어 쓰거나 생략할 수 있다.

2. 선행사에 따른 관계부사의 종류

관계부사 전치사+which	선행사
when (on/at which)	선행사가 시간을 나타내는 말일 때 – the time, the day, the week 등 **Do you remember the day? + We first met then.** → Do you remember <u>the day</u> **when** we first met? 우리가 처음으로 만난 날을 기억하니?
where (in/at which)	선행사가 장소를 나타내는 말일 때 – the place, the room, the house 등 **That is the school. + We used to study there.** → That is <u>the school</u> **where** we used to study. 저것이 우리가 공부했던 학교이다.
why (for which)	선행사가 이유를 나타내는 말일 때 – the reason **Tell me the reason. + She was absent from school for that reason.** → Tell me <u>the reason</u> **why** she was absent from school. 그녀가 학교에 결석한 이유를 말해줘.
how (in which)	선행사가 방법을 나타내는 말일 때 – the way *주의 : 관계부사 how를 쓸 경우 선행사 the way나 관계부사 how 둘 중 하나는 반드시 생략해야 한다. **This is the way. + I study English in that way.** → This is (<u>the way</u>) **how** I study English. → This is <u>the way</u> (**how**) I study English. 이것이 내가 영어를 공부하는 방법이다.

3. **관계부사 = 「전치사 + 관계대명사」**

관계부사는 「전치사+관계대명사」로 바꿔 쓸 수 있다. 이때 전치사를 뒤로 보내고 관계대명사 which 또는 that을 쓰거나 관계대명사와 전치사를 생략할 수도 있다.

This is the place. + I was born there(in that place). 여기는 장소이다. 나는 그 곳에서 태어났다.
→ This is the place **where** I was born.
→ This is the place **in which** I was born. *(formal)*
→ This is the place **which(that)** I was born **in**.
→ This is the place I was born. *(informal)* 여기는 내가 태어난 장소이다.

2005 was the year. + My grandfather passed away then(in that year). 2005년은 해이다. 할아버지가 그때 돌아가셨다.
→ 2005 was the year **when** my grandfather passed away.
→ 2005 was the year **in which** my grandfather passed away. *(formal)*
→ 2005 was the year **which(that)** my grandfather passed away **in**.
→ 2005 was the year my grandfather passed away. *(informal)* 2005년은 할아버지가 돌아가신 해이다.

Unit Test

1. 빈칸에 where, when, why, 또는 how를 써 넣고 아무 것도 필요 없는 곳에는 X표 하시오. 보기를 참고하시오.

> 보기 | This is the place <u>where</u> I live.
> You'll like the way __X__ he teaches.

1. That is the church _____ we were married.
2. Is there a reason _____ you can't come?
3. I like the way _____ he smiles.
4. Will you show me _____ this copy machine works?
5. Do you remember the time _____ you were in the United States?
6. Tell me the reason _____ you were late to class.
7. Do you know the name of the hotel _____ you were staying?
8. I don't like the way _____ she teaches.
9. Sunday is the day _____ we go to church.
10. The place _____ we spent our vacation was really nice.
11. I can't tell you the reason _____ we broke up.
12. The way _____ he smiles is annoying me.

2. 빈칸에 알맞은 말을 보기에서 골라 써 넣으시오.

> 보기 | how he did it   when we got married
> why you left me   which I used to live in

1. This is the house _____
2. Tell me the reason _____
3. 2002 was the year _____
4. I was impressed by _____

3. 우리말과 일치하도록 괄호 안의 단어를 알맞게 배열하시오.

1. 나는 내가 태어난 집을 기억한다. (the house/ I remember/ I was born/ where)

_____

2. 너는 왜 그가 그 돈을 훔쳤는지 아니? (why/ the reason/ do you know/ he stole the money/ ?)

_____

3. 이것이 내가 영어를 공부하는 방법이다. (I study English/ this is/ the way)

_____

4. 너는 네가 여기에 처음 왔던 날을 기억하니? (the day/ do you remember/ when you first came here/ ?)

_____

Writing Pattern Practice | 관계부사

Pattern 1_ 「선행사 + where + 주어 + 동사」

여기가 내가 그를 처음 만난 장소야.(This is the place~)

_____

여기가 학교가 있었던 장소야.(a school used to be)

_____

나는 내가 태어난 집을 기억해.

_____

Pattern 2_ 「선행사 + when + 주어 + 동사」

너는 우리가 처음 만난 날을 기억하니? _____

2002년이 우리가 결혼한 해였다.(get married) _____

일요일은 우리가 교회에 가는 날이다. _____

Pattern 3_ 「선행사 + why + 주어 + 동사」

나는 그녀가 왜 너를 떠났는지 그 이유를 안다. _____

나는 그가 왜 결석했는지 그 이유를 너에게 말할 수 없다.(tell)

_____

너는 왜 그가 그 돈을 훔쳤는지 그 이유를 아니? _____

Pattern 4_ 「the way 생략 + how + 주어 + 동사」 또는 「the way + how 생략 + 주어 + 동사」

이것이 그가 영어를 공부하는 방법이다.(how) _____

나는 그녀가 가르치는 스타일이 좋다.(the way) _____

네가 어떻게 시험에 합격했는지는 미스테리이다.(How~, the exam, a mystery)

_____

64_ 제한적용법/ 계속적용법

● Pattern 　제한적용법: 선행사＋관계대명사절
　계속적용법: 선행사,＋관계대명사절

A: Could you do me a big favor?

B: Sure, what is it?

A: Cindy, who is my friend from California, is looking for an apartment. Since you're an expert, can you help her out?

B: It's the least I can do for you. Any friend of yours is a friend of mine.

1. 관계대명사의 제한적 용법

관계대명사의 제한적 용법은 형용사절이 앞의 선행사를 수식하는 역할을 한다. 보통 제한적 용법에서는 관계대명사가 이끄는 절이 수식하는 명사(선행사)가 누구(무엇)인지 구체적으로 알려주는 역할을 한다. 이 때 관계대명사 앞에 콤마(,)는 없다.

I've got two friends **who** became cooks. 나는 요리사가 된 두 친구가 있다.

2. 관계대명사의 계속적용법

관계대명사가 이끄는 절이 어떤 사람이나 사물에 대한 부가적인 설명을 하는 경우가 있는데, 이를 관계대명사의 계속적용법이라고 한다. 이 때 관계대명사 앞에 콤마(,)를 붙인다.

Cindy, **who** lives next door to Benny, is quite pretty. Cindy는, Benny 옆집에 사는데, 꽤 예뻐.

| MORE TIPS | 제한적용법은 '~한/~된 명사'로 해석하고 계속적용법은 앞에서부터 차례대로 해석한다.
Benny **who** works for Intel~　Intel에 다니는 Benny는~
Benny, **who** works for Intel~　Benny는 Intel에 다니는데~

3. 관계대명사의 두 용법의 비교

● 제한적용법

He loved a woman **who** was a singer. 그는 가수인 여자를 사랑했다.

→ a woman을 '가수가 된 여자'로 제한한다.

● 계속적용법

He loved a woman, **who** became a singer. 그는 여자를 사랑했는데, 그녀가 가수가 되었대.

→ '사랑했던 여자가 있는데 그녀가 가수가 됐고…'라고 하면서 a woman에 관한 내용을 계속 서술해 나가는 느낌이다.

| MORE TIPS 1| 관계대명사 which는 제한적용법이나 계속적용법 모두 사용할 수 있지만 관계대명사 that은 계속적용법에는 사용할 수 없다.

Henry has got a car, **which** costs $30,000.(O) Henry는 차를 가지고 있는데 $30,000 나간다.

Henry has got a car, **that** costs $30,000.(X)

| MORE TIPS 2| 관계대명사 which가 계속적용법으로 쓰인 경우 앞에 있는 문장 전체 내용을 나타내기도 한다.

It rained all day, **which** was good for the garden. 하루 종일 비가 왔는데, 그것은 정원에 도움이 되었다.

Sarah said she was sick, **which** was a lie. Sarah는 아팠다고 말했는데, 그것은 거짓말이었다.

4. 관계부사의 제한적용법과 계속적용법

I went to Busan **where** I was born. 내가 태어난 곳인 부산에 갔다.

→ Busan을 '내가 태어난 곳' 으로 제한한다.

I went to Busan **, where** I stayed there for a month. 나는 부산에 갔다. 그리고 그곳에서 한 달간 머물렀다.

→ 'Busan에 갔는데 한 달 동안 머물렀다.' 라면서 Busan에 관한 내용을 서술해 나가는 느낌이다.

Unit Test

1. 우리말과 일치하도록 빈칸에 알맞은 말을 써 넣으시오. 그리고 콤마(,)가 필요한 경우 □안에 써 넣고, 필요 없는 경우 X표 하시오.

1. 그 노부부에겐 의사인 아들이 있었다.

   The old couple had a son□ _____ was a doctor.

2. 그 노부부에겐 아들이 있는데, 그는 의사가 되었다.

   The old couple had a son□ _____ became a doctor.

3. 그는 꽤 이상해. 그걸 보면 왜 아직도 싱글인지 설명이 되지.

   He is quite strange□ _____ explains why he is still a single.

4. Kate는, 내 상사인데, 정말 지루하다.

   Kate□ _____ is my boss□ is really boring.

5. 그녀는 임신 중이야, 그건 Denny가 곧 아빠가 될 거라는 것을 뜻하지.

   She's expecting a baby□ _____ means that Denny is going to be a father soon.

6. 손상된 그 그림은 Chris에게 팔렸다.

   The picture□ _____ was damaged was sold to Chris.

7. 할아버지가 피자를 주문하셨는데, 그것은 나에게 놀라운 일이었다.

   Grandpa ordered a pizza□ _____ was a surprise to me.

8. 그는 나에게 그의 책을 돌려달라고 했는데, 못 찾겠다.

   He asked me to give him back his book□ _____ I couldn't find.

2. 우리말과 일치하도록 괄호 안의 단어를 알맞게 배열하시오.

1. David은 나와 같이 일하는데, 꽤 웃기다. (,/ ,/ who works with me/ David/ is quite funny.)

   _____

2. 그는 매일 조깅을 하는데, 이것이 그를 건강하게 유지시켜준다. (,/ which/ he goes jogging everyday/ keeps him healthy)

   _____

3. 나는 이태리에 살고 있는 친구가 있다. (I/ who lives in Italy/ have a friend)

   _____

4. 그녀는 스트레스 관리에 관한 책을 썼는데, 난 그 책을 추천해. (I recommend/ ,/ on stress management/ she wrote a book/ which)

   _____

5. 내가 태어난 곳인 부산에 갔다. (I went to Busan/ I was born/ where)

   _____

6. 나는 부산에 갔는데, 그곳에서 한 달간 머물렀다. (I went to Busan/ I stayed there for a month/ ,/ where)

   _____

Writing Pattern Practice | 제한적용법/ 계속적용법

Pattern 1_ 「선행사 + 관계대명사」 제한적 용법

나는 요리사가 된 두 친구가 있다. _____

그에게는 가수가 된 딸이 있다.(He had~) _____

나는 이태리에 살고 있는 친구가 있다. _____

Pattern 2_ 「선행사 + , + 관계대명사」 계속적용법

Cindy는, Benny 옆집에 사는데, 꽤 예뻐.(quire) _____

Kate는, 내 상사인데, 정말 지루하다. _____

그에게는 딸이 하나 있는데, 걔가 가수가 되었대. _____

Sarah는 아팠다고 말했는데, 그것은 거짓말이었다. _____

할아버지가 피자를 주문하셨는데, 그것은 나에게 놀라운 일이었다.(a surprise)

_____

그는 매일 조깅을 하는데, 이것이 그를 건강하게 유지시켜준다.(keep)

_____

Pattern 3_ 「선행사 + 관계부사」 제한적 용법

나는 내가 태어난 곳인 부산에 갔다. _____

우리가 살고 있는 곳은 정말 아름답다.(so) _____

Pattern 4_ 「선행사 + , + 관계부사」 계속적용법

나는 부산에 갔는데, 그곳에서 한 달간 머물렀다. _____

나는 Seattle에 머물렀는데, 그곳에서 몇 년 동안 공부했었다.(used to)

_____

Unit

65 복합관계대명사/ 복합관계부사

● Pattern	관계대명사 + ever –	who(m)ever, whichever whoever, whatever
	관계부사 + ever –	wherever, whenever however

Grammar in Practice

A: I rented a horror movie. Do you want to join us?

B: Sounds good.

A: I also rented a very romantic one.

B: Let's see the scary one. However scary it is, it doesn't matter. How long does the movie run?

A: It's roughly two and a half hours.

Grammar in Use

1. 복합관계대명사

복합관계대명사는 「관계대명사 + ever」의 형태로 선행사 역할과 관계대명사 역할을 동시에 한다. 따라서 복합관계대명사절은 형용사절이 아니라 명사절 또는 부사절로 사용되며 '~든지' 또는 '~일지라도' 의 뜻으로 쓰인다.

2. 명사절을 이끄는 복합관계대명사의 격

(포함된) 선행사	주격	목적격	소유격
사람	whoever (=anyone who)	whomever (=anyone whom)	whosever (=anyone whose)
사물(선택)	whichever (=anything which)	whichever (=anything which/ that)	X
사물(전부)	whatever (=all that)	whatever (=all that)	X

3. 복합관계대명사절 (명사절 역할)

- 주어 역할

  Whoever wants to pass the exam must study hard. 시험에 합격하고 싶은 사람은 누구나 열심히 공부해야 한다.

- 목적어 역할

  Give it to **whomever you like.** 네가 좋아하는 아무나에게 그것을 줘라.

  Choose **whichever you want.** 네가 원하는 어느 것이나 골라라.

  I will give you **whatever you need.** 네가 필요한 무엇이든지 줄게.

- 보어 역할

  A wizard can become **whatever he wants**. 마법사는 원하는 무엇으로나 변환할 수 있다.

4. 부사절을 이끄는 복합관계대명사의 격

(포함된) 선행사	주격	목적격	소유격
사람	whoever (=no matter who)	whomever (=no matter whom)	whosever (=no matter whose)
사물(선택)	whichever (=no matter which)	whichever (=no matter which/ that)	X
사물(전부)	whatever (=no matter what)	whatever (=no matter what)	X

5. 복합관계대명사절 (부사절 역할)

- whoever + 동사/ whomever + 주어 + 동사/ whosever + 주어 + 동사

  Whoever (=No matter who) may come to the party, I'll be glad.

  어느 누가 파티에 오더라도, 나는 기쁠 것이다.

- whichever + 동사/ whichever + 주어 + 동사

  Whichever(No matter which) you may choose, you'll be satisfied. 어느 것을 고르더라도, 당신은 만족할 것입니다.

- whatever + 동사/ whatever + 주어 + 동사

  Whatever(No matter what) you did, I don't care about it. 네가 무엇을 했던 나는 상관하지 않는다.

| MORE TIPS | 복합관계대명사절의 쓰임이 명사절인지 부사절인지 구분하는 방법을 알아보자. 명사절로 쓰였을 경우는 문장 안에서 주어, 목적어, 보어 등 역할을 하는 반면, 부사절로 쓰였을 경우 삭제해도 문장이 성립할 수 있다는 차이로 구분할 수 있다.
You can take **whatever you like.** (명사절) 네가 좋아하는 어느 것이든 가져가.
Whatever you may say, I'll be here for you. (부사절) 네가 뭐라고 말하든, 내가 여기에 있을게.

6. 복합관계부사

복합관계부사는 「관계부사 + ever」의 형태로, 복합관계부사가 이끄는 절은 양보부사절로 사용된다. 복합관계부사에는 wherever, whenever, however 세 가지가 있다.

- Wherever + 주어 + 동사 '어디로(에) ~하더라도'

  Wherever(=No matter where) you go, I will be with you. 네가 어디를 가더라도, 너와 함께 갈 거야.

- Whenever + 주어 + 동사 '언제 ~하더라도'

  Whenever(=No matter when) you come, I'll be pleased. 네가 언제 오던지, 나는 기쁠 거야.

- However + 주어 + 동사 '얼마나/아무리 ~하더라도'

  However(No matter how) tired you may be, you must do it. 네가 아무리 피곤해도, 그것을 해야만 된다.

Unit Test

1. 밑줄친 부분이 명사절이면 '명' 부사절이면 '부' 라고 써 넣으시오.

1. <u>Whoever called just now</u> was very impolite. (　　)
2. <u>Whatever you do</u>, I'll always love you. (　　)
3. <u>Whatever happens</u>, keep calm. (　　)
4. Spend your money on <u>whatever you like</u>. (　　)
5. <u>Whoever may come to the party</u>, I'll be glad. (　　)
6. <u>Whoever you marry</u>, make sure she can cook. (　　)
7. <u>Whoever directed this film</u>, it's not a good one. (　　)
8. I'll go out with <u>whomever I like</u>. (　　)
9. <u>Whatever you say</u>, I don't think she's a nice person. (　　)
10. <u>Whichever you take</u>, you will be satisfied with its quality. (　　)

2. 우리말과 일치하도록 괄호 안의 단어를 알맞게 배열하시오.

1. 시험에 합격하고 싶은 사람은 누구나 열심히 공부해야 한다. (wants to pass the exam/ must study hard/ whoever)

_____

2. 네가 원하는 것은 아무 것이나 골라라. (you want/ whichever/ choose)

_____

3. 네가 필요한 것은 무엇이든지 줄게. (whatever/ I'll give you/ you need)

_____

4. 무슨 일이 있어도, 침착해. (happens/ keep calm/ whatever)

_____

5. 네가 어디를 가더라도, 너와 함께 갈 거야. (I'll be with you/ wherever/ you go)

_____

6. 네가 언제 오던지, 나는 기쁠 거야. (whenever/ I will be pleased/ you come)

_____

7. 아무리 멀어도, 너는 가야 돼. (however/ you must go/ far it may be)

_____

8. 네가 좋아하는 아무에게나 그것을 줘. (whomever/ give it to/ you like)

_____

Writing Pattern Practice | 복합관계대명사/ 복합관계부사

Pattern 1_ 「복합관계대명사절 + 동사」 – 복합관계대명사절 : 명사절(주어)역할

시험에 합격하고 싶은 사람은 누구나 열심히 공부해야 한다.(pass, the exam)

_____

어느 누가 파티에 오더라도, 나는 기쁠 것이다.(may, glad)

_____

Pattern 2_ 「주어 + 동사 + 복합관계대명사절」 – 복합관계대명사절 : 명사절(목적어)역할

네가 좋아하는 아무나에게 그것을 줘라.   _____

네가 원하는 어느 것이나 골라라.   _____

내가 네가 필요한 무엇이든지 줄게.   _____

너는 네가 좋아하는 어느 것이든 가져가도 돼.(take)_____

Pattern 3_ 「주어 + 2형식동사 + 복합관계대명사절」 – 복합관계대명사절 : 명사절(보어)역할

마법사는 원하는 무엇으로나 변할 수 있다.(A wizard) _____

Pattern 4_ 「복합관계대명사절 + 문장」 – 복합관계대명사절 : 부사절역할

무슨 일이 생기든, 나는 네 편이야.(on one's side) _____

어느 것을 고르더라도, 당신은 만족할 것입니다.(Whichever~, may)

_____

네가 무엇을 했던 나는 그것에 대해 상관하지 않는다.(care)

_____

Pattern 5_ 「복합관계부사절 + 문장」 – 복합관계부사절 : 부사절역할

네가 어디를 가던 지, Star Bucks를 발견할 거야. _____

네가 아무리 피곤해도, 그것을 해야만 된다. (may) _____

네가 언제 오더라도 나는 기쁠 것이다.(pleased) _____

66_ 시간/ 조건의 부사절

● Pattern　종속접속사 + 주어 + 동사, 주어 + 동사
　　　　　　주어 + 동사 + 종속접속사 + 주어 + 동사

Grammar in Practice

A: Why don't you have another sandwich?
B: Thanks, but I really can't eat any more.
A: You're going to have dessert, aren't you?
B: Well, I'll join you if you're having something.

Grammar in Use

1. **부사절과 종속접속사**

   부사절은 대부분 앞 또는 뒤에 위치한 주절 전체를 수식하는 역할을 한다. 부사절을 이끄는 종속접속사에는 한 단어로 이루어진 접속사와 두 단어 이상으로 이루어진 접속사구가 있다.
   When you were born, I was 15. 네가 태어났을 때, 나는 15살이었다. (접속사)
   I will leave here **as soon as** the vacation begins. 방학이 시작되자마자 나는 여기를 떠날 거야. (접속사구)

2. **시간 부사절을 이끄는 종속접속사**

   *시간 부사절에서는 현재시제가 미래시제를 대신한다는 점을 유의한다.

   ● 접속사

when ~할 때	as ~할 때	while ~하는 동안	before ~하기 전에
after ~한 후에	since ~한 이래로	once 일단 ~하면	until ~ 때 까지

   Give me a call **when** he comes back. 그가 돌아오면 나에게 전화 줘.
   As I was taking a shower, the phone rang. 내가 샤워하는 중에, 전화가 울렸다.
   You should brush your teeth **before** you go to bed. 잠자리에 들기 전에 이를 닦아야해.
   While you were sleeping, Kate stopped by. 네가 잠든 동안에 Kate가 들렀었어.

   ● 접속사구

as soon as ~하자마자	as long as ~하는 동안, ~하는 한　by the time ~ 때 까지

   I'll get back to you **as soon as** I come back. 돌아오는 즉시 다시 연락드릴께요.
   I don't care about money **as long as** you love me. 네가 나를 사랑하기만 한다면 돈은 상관없어.

I MORE TIPS I until(till)과 by the time은 둘 다 '~할 때까지'로 해석되지만 until은 동작이나 상태가 '~할 때까지' 계속될 때 사용하고 by the time은 기한이 완료됨을 뜻한다.
I'll be waiting here **until** he shows up. 그가 나타날 때까지 여기에서 기다리고 있을 거야.
This assignment should be finished **by the time** school starts. 이 과제는 학교가 시작할 때 까지는 끝마쳐져야 한다.

3. 조건 부사절을 이끄는 종속접속사

* 조건 부사절에서는 현재시제가 미래시제를 대신한다는 점을 유의한다.

● 접속사

if 만약~라면   unless 만약~하지 않는다면(=if ~not)

If it snows tomorrow, I'll go skiing. 내일 눈 오면 스키 타러 갈 거야.
Come tomorrow **unless** I call.(=Come tomorrow **if I don't** call.) 내가 전화하지 않으면 내일 와.

● 접속사구

in case ~인 경우를 대비하여, 만일 ~라면   as far as ~하는 한

In case it rains, you should take your umbrella. 비가 올 경우를 대비해서 너는 우산을 가져가는 게 좋아.
As far as I know, she is very nice. 내가 아는 한 그녀는 매우 좋은 사람이다.

Unit Test

1. 우리말과 일치하도록 괄호 안에 알맞은 말을 보기에서 골라 써 넣으시오.

보기 | until   if   unless   in case   by the time   before   when

1. 네가 아플 경우를 대비해서 약을 가져가야 돼.
_____ you get sick, you should take some medicine.
2. 내가 전화하지 않으면 내일 와.
Come tomorrow _____ I call.
3. 만약 내일 날씨가 화창하다면, 우리는 피크닉 갈 거야.
_____ it's sunny tomorrow, we'll go on a picnic.
4. 날씨가 나아질 때 시골에서 주말을 보내자.
Let's have a weekend in the country _____ the weather gets better.
5. 너는 일본으로 돌아가기 전에 Paul을 만나야 해.
You must see Paul _____ you go back to Japan.
6. 그가 나타날 때까지 여기에서 앉아 있을 거야.
I'll be sitting here _____ he shows up.
7. 이 책은 도서관 문 닫을 때까지 반납되어야 한다.
This book must be returned _____ the library closes.

2. 의미가 자연스러워지도록 주어진 문장 뒤에 올 수 있는 것을 골라 연결하시오.

1. When she comes home   ⓐ you should turn off the lights
2. In case it rains   ⓑ he's a very boring person
3. As far as I know   ⓒ give me a call.
4. Before you go out   ⓓ you should take an umbrella.
5. He worked as a salesman   ⓔ when he was in his 20s.
6. You can go out   ⓕ as long as you tell me where you're going.

3. 틀린 곳을 찾아 밑줄치고 고쳐 쓰시오.

1. If it will rain tomorrow, I'll just stay home.
→ _____
2. Let's buy a bottle of wine in case Roger will come.
→ _____
3. I have to be here until he will fall asleep.
→ _____
4. If you two will have a fight, I'll be on your side.
→ _____

Writing Pattern Practice | 시간/ 조건의 부사절

Pattern 1_ 「when /while /before /after /since /once /until/ as soon as/ by the time + 주어 + 동사」 시간
부사절을 이끄는 종속접속사

그가 돌아오면 나에게 전화 줘.(Give~, when) _____

내가 샤워하고 있었을 때, 전화가 울렸다.(As~) _____

너는 잠자리에 들기 전에 이를 닦아야 해.(You should~) _____

네가 잠든 동안에 Kate가 들렀어.(While~, stop by) _____

내가 한국에 도착하자마자 너에게 들를게.(I'll visit~) _____

네가 나를 사랑하기만 한다면 돈은 상관없어.(I don't~) _____

_____

그가 나타날 때까지 여기에서 기다리고 있을 거야.(I'll be~, show up) _____

_____

그는 결혼하기 전에 기계공으로 일했다.(Before~, a mechanic) _____

_____

그녀는 학교를 마치고 중국으로 갔다. _____

Pattern 2_ 「if/ unless/ in case/ as far as + 주어 + 동사」 조건 부사절을 이끄는 종속접속사

네가 오면 나는 기쁠 거야.(glad) _____

눈이 오지 않으면 내가 거기에 갈게요.(I'll be~) _____

비가 올 경우를 대비해서 너는 우산을 가져가는 게 좋아.(should) _____

_____

내가 아는 한 그녀는 매우 좋은 사람이다.(very nice) _____

_____

124

Unit

67 이유/ 양보/ 결과의 부사절

● **Pattern**　종속접속사 + 주어 + 동사, 주어 + 동사

　　　　　　　주어 + 동사 + 종속접속사 + 주어 + 동사

A: Do you have any plans for this weekend?

B: I need to go shopping for Christmas presents.

A: I envy you. I'll be working this weekend, too. Christmas is just around the corner, though.

B: Poor you.

1.　이유 부사절을 이끄는 종속접속사

● 접속사

> ~ 때문에
> **because** (~때문에, 비교적 강한 이유)　　　**as** (~때문에, 구어체)
> **since** (~이므로, 당연히 알만한 이유)　　　**for** (~때문에, 문어체)

I couldn't feel anger against him **because** I like him so much. 나는 그를 너무 좋아해서 그에게 화를 낼 수가 없었다.

I didn't know that she had been married **as** she seldom talked about herself. 그녀가 그녀 자신에 대해 얘기하는 경우가 드물어 그녀가 결혼했었다는 것을 나는 알지 못했다.

Since it was getting dark, we had to go home. 점점 어두워졌으므로 우리는 집으로 가야만 했다.

● 접속사구

> **now that** ~하기 때문에, ~한 이상 (비교적 가벼운 이유)

Now that we have eaten, let's go. 이제 먹었으니까 출발하자.

2.　양보 부사절을 이끄는 종속접속사

● 접속사(구)

> 비록 ~이지만
> **(al)though**　**(even) if**　**even though** (비교적 강한 양보의 의미)

Though he is 8 years old, he speaks five languages. 그가 8살임에도 불구하고 5개 국 언어를 말할 수 있다.

I loved the story **even though** it was totally fictitious.
비록 완전히 꾸며낸 것일지라도, 나는 그 이야기가 마음에 들었다.

I MORE TIPS I He speaks five languages. He is 8 years old, **though**. *회화체에서 though를 맨 뒤로 보내 '그러나(but)'의 뜻으로 쓰기도 한다.

3. 목적 부사절을 이끄는 종속접속사

● 접속사(구)

> (so) that + 주어 + may(can) + 동사원형 : ~하기 위하여
>
> in order that + 주어 + may(can) + 동사원형 : ~하기 위하여 *문어적 표현
>
> lest + 주어 + (should) + 동사원형 : ~하지 않기 위하여 *문어적 표현

I'll give you the key **so that** you **can** unlock the door. 네가 문을 열 수 있도록 열쇠를 줄게.

They met on Saturdays **in order that** everybody might be free to attend.
그들은 모두가 참석할 수 있도록 하기 위해 토요일마다 만났다.

4. 결과 부사절을 이끄는 종속접속사

● 접속사(구)

> so + 형용사/부사 + that + 주어 + 동사 : 매우 '형용사/부사' 해서 결국 ~하다
>
> such + (관사) + (형용사) + 명사 + that + 주어 + 동사 : 매우 ~한 명사라서 결국 ~하다

Susie is **so** kind **that** everybody likes her. Susie는 매우 친절해서 모두가 그녀를 좋아한다.

Susie is **such** a kind person **that** everybody likes her. Susie는 매우 친절한 사람이라서 모두가 그녀를 좋아한다.

● – As의 다양한 쓰임 | Grammar Point |

• ~할 때
  As I was studying, the doorbell rang. 공부하고 있었을 때 초인종이 울렸다.

• ~이기/하기 때문에
  As it was very hot and humid, we didn't go outside.

• ~인 것과/~한 것과 같이
  Don't lose your passport **as** I did last year.

• ~함에 따라
  As he grows old, he gets more handsome. 그는 나이가 듦에 따라 더욱 잘생겨진다.

Unit Test

1. 우리말과 일치하도록 괄호 안에 알맞은 말을 보기에서 골라 써 넣으시오. (중복사용 불가능)

| 보기 | so that   so~that   because   although   such~that   though |

1. 비록 그가 거짓말을 했지만 나는 그를 용서했다.
   _____ he told a lie, I forgave him.
2. 교통 혼잡에 걸리지 않기 위하여 나는 일찍 출발할 것이다.
   I'm going to make an early start _____ I don't get stuck in the traffic jam.
3. 날씨가 너무 안 좋아서 나는 집에 머물러야 했다.
   The weather was _____ bad _____ I had to stay home.
4. 그는 매우 좋은 사람이어서 나는 그가 내 친구가 되기를 원했다.
   He was _____ a nice person _____ I wanted him to be my friend.
5. 그가 너무 화를 내서 우리는 그에게 말을 할 수 없었다.
   _____ he was too angry, I couldn't speak to him.
6. 나는 태국 음식을 좋아한다. 매우 맵지만.
   I like Thai food. It's very spicy, _____ .

2. 의미가 자연스러워지도록 주어진 문장 뒤에 올 수 있는 것을 골라 연결하시오.

1. Because she was mad at me,   ⓐ he went to work.
2. I took my golf club   ⓑ I went to go home early.
3. Although he was tired,   ⓒ He doesn't have much money, though.
4. Since I was tired,   ⓓ so that I could play at the weekend.
5. I like him very much.   ⓔ she didn't even say hello to me.

3. 우리말과 일치하도록 괄호 안의 단어를 알맞게 배열하시오.

1. 비록 그가 성질은 고약했지만 친구는 많았다. (he had lots of friends/ although/ he was bad-tempered)

_____

2. 점점 어두워졌으므로 우리는 집으로 가야만 했다. (since/ we had to go home/ it was getting dark)

_____

3. 그는 너무 조용히 이야기를 해서 우리가 그와 말할 수 없었다. (we couldn't talk to him/ that/ he talked/ so quietly)

_____

4. 그는 훌륭한 학생이어서 토익시험에서 높은 점수를 받았다. (he got a high score on the TOEIC test/ such a good student/ he is/ that)

_____

Writing Pattern Practice | 이유/ 양보/ 결과의 부사절

Pattern 1_ 「because/ since/ as/ for/ now that + 주어 + 동사」 이유 부사절을 이끄는 종속접속사

나는 그에게 화가 났기 때문에 그와 말하고 싶지 않았다.(Because~, mad at, talk to)

_____

점점 어두워졌으므로 우리는 집으로 가야만 했다.(Since~)

_____

기말고사가 끝난 이상, 나는 친구들과 재미있게 보낼 수 있다.(the finals are over, have fun)

_____

Pattern 2_ 「(al)though/ (even) if/ even though + 주어 + 동사」 양보 부사절을 이끄는 종속접속사

그가 여덟 살임에도 불구하고 5개국 언어를 말할 수 있다.(Though~, speak)

_____

그 이야기가 비록 완전히 꾸며낸 것일지라도, 나는 그 이야기가 마음에 들었다.(I loved~, totally fictitious)

_____

Pattern 3_ 「(so) that + 주어 + may(can) + 동사원형」, 「in order that + 주어 + may(can) + 동사원형」, 「lest + 주어 + (should) + 동사원형」 목적 부사절을 이끄는 종속접속사

네가 문을 열 수 있도록 열쇠를 줄게.(I'll~, so that, unlock)

_____

지금 시작하자, 우리가 충분한 시간을 가질 수 있게.(so that, enough)

_____

Pattern 4_ 「so + 형용사/부사 + that + 주어 + 동사」, 「such + (관사) + (형용사) + 명사 + that + 주어 + 동사」 결과 부사절을 이끄는 종속접속사

Susie는 매우 친절해서 모두가 그녀를 좋아한다.(so)

_____

Susie는 매우 친절한 사람이라서 모두가 그녀를 좋아한다.(such)

_____

Unit

68_ 가정법

● **Pattern** If절, + 주절
주절 + if절

A: I'm sorry that I was late last night. I was tied up at work.
B: If I were you, I wouldn't lie like that. I know you were drinking last night.
A: That's *absurd. What makes you say that?
B: Brad saw you at the bar.

*absurd 터무니없는, 불합리한

1. **가정법**

● **조건의 가정법** – 어떤 조건이 주어졌을 때 앞으로 일어나게 될 상황을 나타내는 경우 '조건의 가정법'을 쓴다. 이때 if절 동사는 현재, 앞으로 벌어질 상황을 나타내는 주절은 보통 미래동사 또는 「can+동사원형」을 쓴다.

If you **stop** smoking, I**'ll marry** you. 담배 끊으면 결혼할게.

● **상상의 가정법** – 조건의 가정법을 제외하면 나머지는 보통 '상상의 가정법'에 해당된다. 실제 상황과 다른 불가능한 일을 상상하거나 소망할 때 사용한다.

If I **had** more money, I **would travel** to Europe. 돈이 더 있으면 유럽으로 여행갈텐데.

2. **가정법 미래**

미래에 어떤 일이 일어날 가능성이 있을 때 가정법미래를 쓰는데, 어떤 일이 일어날 가능성이 적을 경우 if절에 should를 쓰고 불가능한 것을 가정할 때는 were/was to를 쓴다.

> 「If + 주어 + 현재형동사, 주어 + will/can + 동사원형」 '~하면 …할 거야'

If you **get** here before eight, we **can catch** the train. 네가 8시 전에 여기에 도착하면, 우리는 기차를 탈 수 있을 텐데.

> 「If + 주어 + should + 동사원형, 주어 + will/can + 동사원형」 '혹시~하면 …할 거야'
> 「If + 주어 + were/was to + 동사원형, 주어 + would/could + 동사원형」 '혹시~하면 …할 거야'

If you **should run into** Ted, **tell** him to call me. 혹시 Ted를 우연히 만나면, 내게 전화하라고 말해.
If you **should happen** to finish early, **give** me a ring. 혹시 일찍 끝마치게 되면, 전화 줘.
If I **were to be** a student again, I **would study** music. 만약 다시 학생이 된다면, 음악을 공부할 텐데.

I MORE TIPS I 가정법 미래의 경우 주절에 will/can 대신, 상황에 따라 would, should, could, might 등을 쓸 수 있다.
If you jog everyday, you **might** lose your weight. 네가 매일 조깅을 하면 몸무게가 줄 거야.
If you should happen to meet Sally, perhaps you **could** say hello to her. 혹시 Sally를 만나게 되면, 인사 전해줘.

3. 가정법 과거

가정법 과거시제는 '현재'의 사실에 반대되거나 어긋날 때 사용된다. if절의 be동사는 대부분 were을 쓰지만 was를 쓰는 경우도 있다.

> 「If + 주어 + 과거형동사, 주어 + would/could + 동사원형」 '(현재에)~라면 …할 텐데'

If I were rich, **I would** spend all my time travelling. 내가 부자라면 모든 시간을 여행하면서 보낼 텐데. (=As I'm not rich, I can't spend all my time travelling)

*If I were you~는 상대방에게 충고할 때 주로 쓴다.
If I were you, **I'd** get that car serviced. 내가 너라면 자동차 점검 받을 텐데. *would나 could를 'd로 쓰거나 말하기도 한다.

4. 가정법 과거완료

가정법과거시제는 '과거'의 사실에 반대되거나 어긋날 때 사용된다.

> 「If + 주어 + 과거완료, 주어 + would/could + have + 과거분사」 '(과거에)~했다면 …했을 텐데'

If John **had played** well, the team **would have** won. John이 잘 뛰었다면 팀이 승리했을 텐데. (=As John didn't play well, the team didn't win.)

5. 혼합 가정법

형태상 if절에는 과거완료 동사가, 주절에는 과거동사가 오는 것을 혼합 가정법이라고 한다. 따라서 '과거'의 사실에 반대되거나 어긋나는 가정을 하고, 그 결과 '현재'의 사실과 다른 상상을 하는 상황으로 내용상 과거와 현재가 혼합된 형태이다.

> 「If + 주어 + 과거완료, 주어 + would/could + 동사원형」 '(과거에)~했다면 …(현재) 할 텐데'

If I had finished my report yesterday, **I could** hang out with my friends now. 어제 보고서를 끝냈더라면 지금 친구와 놀 수 있을 텐데. (=As I didn't finish my report yesterday, I can't hang out with my friends.)

● 가정법 정리			Grammar Point	
종류	**실제시제**	**형태**
가정법 미래	미래	If + 주어 + 현재형동사, 주어 + will/can + 동사원형 If + 주어 + should + 동사원형, 주어 + will/can + 동사원형 If + 주어 + was/were to + 동사원형, 주어 + will/can + 동사원형
가정법 과거	현재	If + 주어 + 과거형동사, 주어 + would/could + 동사원형
가정법 과거완료	과거	If + 주어 + 과거완료, 주어 + would/could + have + 과거분사
혼합 가정법	과거+현재	If + 주어 + 과거완료, 주어 + would/could + 동사원형

Unit Test

1. 괄호 안의 단어를 '현재시제' 또는 'will + 동사원형' 중 골라 알맞은 형태로 써 넣으시오.

1. If I _____ (have) enough time tomorrow, I _____ (visit) you.
2. Helen _____ (be) sorry if you _____ (not come)
3. If you _____ (wash) up, I _____ (dry)
4. If you _____ (help) me with my homework, I _____ (finish) earlier.
5. If I _____ (see) him, I _____ (ask) his phone number.
6. We _____ (be) happy if you _____ (come) and join us.
7. If Denny _____ (not come) late, we _____ (go) out for dinner.

2. 보기와 같이 각자의 생각을 적어보시오.

> 보기 | I'll be sad if my English doesn't get better.

1. I'll be happy_____.
2. I'll be sorry_____.
3. I'll be bored_____.

3. 우리말과 일치하도록 괄호 안에 알맞은 말을 써 넣으시오.

1. 내가 돈이 충분하다면, 하와이로 여행갈 텐데.
   If I _____ enough money, I _____ travel to Hawaii.
2. 내가 의사선생님이라면, 너를 도와줄 수 있을 텐데.
   If I _____ a doctor, I _____ help you.
3. 네가 최선을 다했더라면, 실패하지 않았을 텐데.
   If you _____ your best, I wouldn't _____ _____.
4. 그가 Laura와 결혼하지 않았더라면, 그는 아직도 미혼일 텐데.
   If he _____ not married Laura, he _____ be still single.
5. 혹시 Terry를 우연히 만나면, 나에게 전화하라고 말해.
   If you _____ run into Terry, tell him to call me.
6. 네가 덜 먹는다면, 몸무게를 줄일 수 있을 텐데.
   If you _____ less, you _____ lose your weight.
7. 내가 너라면, 그것을 하지 않을 텐데.
   If I _____ you, I _____ not do that.
8. 내가 다시 태어난다면, 공부를 열심히 할 텐데.
   If I _____ _____ be born again, I _____ study hard.

Writing Pattern Practice | 가정법

Pattern 1_ 가정법 미래

「If + 주어 + 현재형동사, 주어 + will/can + 동사원형」 '~하면 …할 거야'

네가 8시 전에 여기에 도착하면, 우리는 기차를 잡을 수 있을 텐데.(get, catch)

_____

「If + 주어 + should + 동사원형, 주어 + will/can + 동사원형」 '혹시~하면 …할 거야'

혹시 네가 Terry를 우연히 만나면, 나에게 전화하라고 말해.(run into, tell~to)

_____

「If + 주어 + were/was to + 동사원형, 주어 + would/could + 동사원형」 '혹시~하면 …할 거야'

내가 만약 다시 학생이 된다면, 음악을 공부할 텐데. _____

Pattern 2_ 가정법 과거

「If + 주어 + 과거형동사, 주어 + would/could + 동사원형」 '(현재에)~라면 …할 텐데'

내가 부자라면, 저 차를 살 수 있을 텐데. _____

내가 너라면, 거기에 안갈 텐데. _____

내가 차가 있다면, 너를 더 자주 보러갈 수 있을 텐데.(go to see)

_____

Pattern 3_ 가정법 과거완료

「If + 주어 + 과거완료, 주어 + would/could + have + 과거분사」 '(과거에)~했다면 …했을 텐데'

John이 잘 뛰었다면, 팀이 승리했을 텐데.(play) _____

내가 너의 전화번호를 알았더라면, 네게 전화할 수 있었을 텐데.

_____

Pattern 4_ 혼합 가정법

「If + 주어 + 과거완료, 주어 + would/could + 동사원형」 '(과거에)~했다면 (현재에) …할 텐데'

내가 어제 보고서를 끝냈더라면, 지금 친구와 놀 수 있을 텐데.(hang out with)

_____

Unit

69_ 가정법의 응용

● Pattern
I wish+가정법
as if+가정법,
It's time+주어+동사

A: I think it's about time we got going.

B: Already? Won't you have some more coffee?

A: I'd love to, but I'm supposed to get up early tomorrow morning.

B: Oh! I'm sorry. I wish you could stay **a little longer.**

---

1. I wish+가정법

● I wish+가정법 과거

'현재' 사실과 다른 상황을 소원할 때 사용하며 「I wish + 주어 + 동사의 과거형」 형태로, 뜻은 '~한다면 좋을 텐데' 이다.

I wish I could speak Chinese. 중국어를 할 수 있다면 좋을 텐데. (=I'm sorry that I can't speak Chinese.)

I wish I were in your shoes. 네 입장이라면 좋을 텐데. (=I'm sorry that I'm not in your shoes.)

● I wish+가정법 과거완료

'과거' 사실과 다른 상황을 소원할 때 사용하며 「I wish + 주어 + had + p.p」 형태로, 뜻은 '~했다면 좋았을 텐데' 이다.

I wish Jane had come to my birthday party yesterday. 어제 Jane이 내 생일 파티에 왔었다면 좋았을 텐데. (=I'm sorry that Jane didn't come to my birthday party yesterday.)

I wish I had been there. 내가 거기에 있었더라면 좋았을 텐데. (=I'm sorry that I wasn't there.)

2. as if 가정법

● as if+가정법 과거

'현재' 사실과 다른 상황을 가정할 때 사용하며 「as if + 주어 + 동사의 과거형」 형태로, 뜻은 '마치 ~인 것처럼' 이다.

He talks **as if** he knew everything. 그는 (현재) 마치 자기가 모든 것을 아는 것처럼 말한다.

He talked **as if** he knew everything. 그는 (과거 당시에) 마치 자기가 모든 것을 아는 것처럼 말했다.

● as if + 가정법과거완료

'과거' 사실과 다른 상황을 가정할 때 사용하며 「as if + 주어 + had + p.p」 형태로, 뜻은 '마치~ 였던 것처럼' 이다.

He talks as if he had dated Mary. 그는 (전에) 마치 Mary와 데이트 했던 것처럼 말한다.

He talked as if he had dated Mary. 그는 (그 이전에) 마치 Mary와 데이트 했었던 것처럼 말했다.

3. It's time~ 구문

> 「It's (about) time (that) + 가정법 과거」 '~할 시간이다'

It's time that you went to bed. (지금은) 잠자리에 들 시간이다. (왜 안가고 있니?)

| MORE TIPS | It's time 다음에 과거시제가 아닌 to부정사가 오는 경우 '유감' 을나타내기 보다 단순히 '~할 시간이다' 라 는 의미로 쓰인다.
It is time to have dinner. 저녁먹을 시간이다.

4. if의 생략

if절에서 if가 생략되면, be동사나 조동사는 도치되어 문장의 맨 앞에 오게 된다.

1. if의 생략

● 「If + 주어 + be동사」 → 「Be동사 + 주어」

If I were you, →Were I you,

● 「If + 주어 + 조동사」 → 「조동사 + 주어」

If I should fail the test,→Should I fail the test,

● 「If + 주어 + 일반동사」 → 「Do(es)/ Did + 주어 + 본동사」

If I had a car,→Did I have a car,

2. if를 제외한 다른 표현

● 「Unless + 주어 + 동사~」 '~않는다면'

Unless you do your best,~ 네가 최선을 다하지 않는다면 (=If you don't do your best)

● 「Provided(Providing) + 주어 + 동사~」 '~하기만 한다면', '~라면'

Provided(Providing) he doesn't come with his dog,~ 그가 그의 개와 함께 오지만 않는다면 (=As long as he doesn' t come with his dog,~)

● 「Suppose(Supposing) + 주어 + 동사~」 '가령 ~하면'

Suppose(Supposing) you picked up 10,000 dollars,~ 네가 만약 10,000달러를 줍 는다면 (=If you picked up 10,000 dollars, ~)

Unit Test

1. 보기와 같이 두 문장이 같은 뜻이 되도록 알맞은 말을 써 넣으시오.

> 보기 | I wish I had a BMW.
> → I'm sorry that <u>I don't have a BMW.</u>

1. I wish I had a brother.
→ I'm sorry that _____

2. I wish I were in your shoes.
→ I'm sorry that _____

3. I wish I had enough time.
→ I'm sorry that _____

4. I wish she had come to the meeting.
→ I'm sorry that _____

5. I wish I had been at the party.
→ I'm sorry that _____

2. 보기와 같이 다음 문장의 숨겨진 뜻을 써 넣으시오.

> It's time you went to bed.
> → Why aren't you going to bed?

1. It's time you brushed your teeth.
→ _____

2. It's time you got up.
→ _____

3. It's time you vacuum the floor.
→ _____

3. 둘 중 알맞은 것을 고르시오.

1. We'll have a party outside tomorrow (provided/ unless) it rains.
2. (Unless/ Suppose) you got fired. What would you do?
3. (Provided/ Unless) no one has any further questions, the meeting will be adjourned.

Writing Pattern Practice | 가정법의 응용

Pattern 1_ 「I wish + 주어 + 동사의 과거형」 '~라면 좋을 텐데'

내가 스페인어를 할 수 있다면 좋을 텐데. _____

내가 네 입장이라면 좋을 텐데.(~ in your shoes) _____

Pattern 2_ 「I wish + 주어 + had + p.p」 '~했다면 좋았을 텐데'

어제 Jane이 내 생일 파티에 왔었다면 좋았을 텐데.

_____

내가 거기에 있었더라면 좋았을 텐데. _____

Pattern 3_ 「as if + 주어 + 동사의 과거형」 '마치~인 것처럼'

그는 (현재) 마치 자기가 노인인 것처럼 말한다.(an old man)

_____

그는 (그 당시에) 마치 자기가 노인인 것처럼 말했다. _____

Pattern 4_ 「as if + 주어 + had + p.p」 '마치~였던 것처럼'

그는 (전에) 마치 유령을 본 것처럼 말한다.(a ghost) _____

그는 (그 이전에) 마치 유령을 봤던 것처럼 말했다. _____

Pattern 5_ It's (about) time (that) + 가정법 과거 '~할 시간이다'

네가 잠자리에 들 시간이다. _____

Pattern 6_ if를 제외한 다른 표현

「Unless + 주어 + 동사~ 」 '~않다면'

비가 안 오면, _____

「Provided(Providing) + 주어 + 동사~」 '~하기만 한다면', '~라면'

그가 늦게 오지만 않는다면, _____

「Suppose(Supposing) + 주어 + 동사~」 '가령 ~하면'

네가 만약 10,000달러를 줍는다면, _____

1. 틀린 곳을 찾아 밑줄치고 고쳐 쓰시오.

1. I asked where were the President and his wife staying?
→ _____

2. The first question on the interview was about where did I live.
→ _____

3. Could you tell me what time is it?
→ _____

4. We talked about who was the most important person in our life.
→ _____

5. I'd like to know who did you call.
→ _____

6. Tell me how do you have such a good memory.
→ _____

7. You should always carry your identification card to show who are you.
→ _____

8. I don't know what time does the basketball game begin.
→ _____

9. I wonder if does he have a friend to count on.
→ _____

10. I asked if could he lend me some money.
→ _____

11. The doctor which treated me wasn't very nice.
→ _____

12. I've lost the necklace whose Michael gave me.
→ _____

13. The thing what she said made me upset.
→ _____

14. This is exactly the thing what I wanted to buy.
→ _____

15. Do you want to see the thing what I bought yesterday?
→ _____

2. 둘 중 알맞은 것을 고르시오.

1. The man (whom/ which) I met yesterday is my uncle.
2. He gave me (what/ which) I wanted to buy.
3. 1990 was the year in (which, when) we got married.
4. This is the place in (which, where) I was born.
5. This is the way (how, X) I study English.

3. 빈칸에 알맞은 관계대명사, 또는 관계부사를 쓰시오. (단, that은 제외)

1. Is this the key _____ Jenny was looking for?
2. He lives in a village _____ there are no schools.
3. There's a movie tonight _____ you might like.
4. Do you know the people _____ live upstairs?
5. Do you remember the old lady _____ we met in Paris?
6. People _____ take physical exercise live much longer.
7. It was a message _____ purpose I did not understand.
8. Cindy, _____ is my best friend, has moved to Japan.
9. I married a man _____ I met Canada.
10. Jason, _____ I taught, became a scientist.

※ 빈칸에 들어갈 가장 알맞은 말은?

1. This assignment should be finished _____ school begins.

　① until　　　　　　② since
　③ as long as　　　④ by the time

2. _____ you get sick, you should take some medicine.

　① Until　　　　　② As far as
　③ As long as　　④ In case

3. You can take my car _____ you drive carefully.

　① until　　　　　② as far as
　③ as long as　　④ while

4. We lived in Seattle _____ we were first married.

　① until　　　　　② where
　③ since　　　　　④ by

5. _____ they were playing cards, somebody broke into the house.

　① Until　　　　　② As far as
　③ Since　　　　　④ While

6. We were late _____ it rained.

① because   ② if
③ unless   ④ though

7. I like Kimchi very much. It's hot and spicy, _____

① because   ② if
③ even if   ④ though

8. 둘 중 알맞은 것을 고르시오.

1. If the wether (is/ were) fine, we can go on a picnic this afternoon.
2. Unless it (were/ weren't) snowy, we could go out and play soccer.
3. If I (am/ were) you, I wouldn't do that.
4. If people didn't drive fast, there (can be/ could be) fewer accidents.
5. If I (had been/ were) hungry, I would have eaten something.
6. If I have enough money, I (will buy/ buy) my own house.
7. If I (had known/ knew) his address, I would have visited him.
8. If I were a doctor, I (will/ would) help her.

9. 다음 글을 읽고, 빈칸에 차례로 들어갈 알맞은 말을 고르시오.

You might have seen or read one of the *Harry Potter* series. Harry Potter was an orphan _____ lived with his aunt and uncle. He had spent many years of his life sleeping under the stairs of the family who disliked him.

Harry Potter was a highly unusual boy in many ways. For one thing, he hated the summer holidays more than any other time of year. For another, he discovered that he was a wizard himself! One day on Harry's birthday, he received a letter. Since then, 100 letters has been sent to Harry and they were all invitations to study at Hogwart's Wizard school. It said "We are pleased to inform you that you have been accepted at Hogwart's School of Witchcraft and Wizardry." Harry accepted the invitation and left his aunt and uncle.

This is _____ happens to young Harry Potter in J.K. Rowling's enchanting, funny debut novel, *Harry Potter*. To find out more, you'll have to read the book of see the movie.

① who - that   ② who - what   ③ which - that   ④ which - what

*Chapter 8 | 주의해야 할 용법

70_ 시제일치

● **Pattern** 1. 주어 + 동사 + (시간) 부사 → 시제일치
2. 주절(주어 + 동사) + 종속절(접속사 + 주어 + 동사)
→ 시제일치

A: I think you're really athletic.

B: Yes. I like sports very much. What about you?

A: Well. I don't like sports that are too strenuous. I used to play badminton but I'm a bit *rusty now.

B: Okay. Why don't we play badminton sometime?

*rusty 서투른, 무딘

1. 시제일치

영어에서 시제를 나타낼 수 있는 것은 동사와 부사이다. 그리고 종속절의 동사의 시제가 주절의 동사의 시제에 영향을 받는 경우가 많다. 그러므로 시제일치를 공부하기 위해서는 동사와 부사와의 관계, 그리고 주절 동사와 종속절 동사와의 관계를 잘 살펴야 하겠다.

2. 시제일치의 원칙

● 동사의 시제와 (시간)부사의 시제는 일치시켜야 한다.

Sally **now lives** in New York. Sally는 현재 뉴욕에서 산다.
　　　　현재　현재

David and I **went** out for dinner **last night.** David과 나는 어젯밤 저녁 먹으러 나갔다.
　　　　　　　과거　　　　　　　　　　　　　　　　과거

● 종속절의 시제는 주절의 시제에 영향을 받는다.

주절의 시제가 현재일 경우, 종속절에는 '모든' 시제가 올 수 있다.

I **think** that she **goes** to work. 나는 그녀가 직장에 다닌다고 생각한다.
　현재　　　　　　　현재

I **think** that she **went** to work. 나는 그녀가 직장에 갔다고 생각한다.
　현재　　　　　　　과거

I **think** that she **will go** to work. 나는 그녀가 직장에 갔다고 생각한다.
　현재　　　　　　　미래

● 주절의 시제가 과거일 경우, 종속절에는 대부분 과거나 과거완료동사가 온다. 단, 종속절에 조동사 will, can 등을 쓸 경우 would, could로 바꿔 쓴다.

I **thought** that she **was** busy working. 나는 그녀가 일하느라 바쁘다고 생각했다.
　과거　　　　　　　과거

I **thought** that she **had been** busy working. 나는 그녀가 일하느라 바빴다고 생각했다.
　과거　　　　　　　과거완료

I **thought** that she **would** be busy working. 나는 그녀가 일하느라 바쁠 거라고 생각했다.
　과거　　　　　　　would, could, might 등

3. 시제일치의 예외

- 과학적 사실이나 속담, 반복적인 행위 및 직업 등은 항상 현재시제로만 쓴다.

  The boy **learned** that light <u>travels</u> faster than sound. 소년은 빛이 소리보다 빠르다
  　　　　　과거　　　　　　　　　　　　현재
  는 것을 배웠다.

  Brian **said** that he always <u>exercises</u> in the morning. Brian은 항상 아침에 운동한다고
  　　　　과거　　　　　　　　현재
  말했다.

- 역사적인 사실일 경우 항상 과거시제로만 쓴다.

  We **know** that Caesar <u>was</u> the first Roman emperor. 우리는 시저가 로마제국의 첫
  　　현재　　　　　　　　과거
  번째 황제였다는 것을 안다.

- 시간과 조건을 나타내는 부사절에서는 현재시제가 미래를 대신한다.

  If my brother **comes** back home, I'<u>ll</u> give him a big hug. 동생이 집에 돌아오면
  　　　　　　현재　　　　　　　　미래
  나는 그를 꽉 안아 줄 거야.

- 과거의 상황이 현재에도 지속되는 경우 종속절의 시제는 현재와 과거시제 모두 가능하다.

  Mary **said** that she <u>is</u> single. Mary는 그녀가 미혼이라고 말했다.(지금도 미혼일 경우)
  = Mary **said** that she <u>was</u> single.

Unit Test

1. 다음 문장을 과거문장으로 바꿀 때 빈 칸에 알맞은 말을 써 넣으시오.

1. Ann says that she has a cold.
→ Ann said that _____.
2. Tom says that Kelly has finished her lunch.
→ Tom said that _____.
3. I know that he will give up.
→ I knew that _____.
4. I know that water is made up of hydrogen and oxygen.
→ I know that _____.

2. 틀린 곳을 찾아 밑줄치고 고쳐 쓰시오.

1. Ted said that he may go to Europe in summer.
2. My teacher said that the Civil War breaks out in 1861.
3. People say that haste made waste.
4. Tom said that he always got up before 6 in the morning.
5. Henna said that she will go on a diet.

3. 다음 괄호 안의 단어를 이용하여 시제에 맞게 영작을 완성하시오.

1. 그는 매일 아침식사를 한다고 말했다.
   He said that he _____ (have breakfast) everyday.
2. 나는 네가 아파 누워 있다고 생각했다.
   I thought that you _____ (be sick in bed).
3. 나는 제 2차 세계 대전이 1939년에 일어났다는 것을 몰랐다.
   I didn't know that World War II _____ (break out) in 1939.
4. 그 소년은 지구가 태양을 돈다는 것을 배웠다.
   The boy learned that the Earth _____ (go around) the Sun.
5. 그가 집에 오면 나는 그를 꽉 안아줄 거야.
   If he _____ (come home), I'll give him a hug.

Writing Pattern Practice | 시제일치

Pattern 1_ 동사와 (시간)부사의 시제일치

Sally는 현재 뉴욕에서 산다.(Sally now~)　_____

David과 나는 어젯밤 춤추러 갔었다.　_____

Pattern 2_ 주절이 현재일 때 종속절은 '모든' 시제가능

나는 네가 돈이 좀 필요한 것을 안다.　_____

나는 네가 돈이 좀 필요했던 것을 안다.　_____

나는 네가 돈이 좀 필요할 것을 안다.　_____

Pattern 3_ 주절이 과거, 과거완료시제일 때 종속절도 과거, 과거완료시제

나는 네가 아파서 침대에 있다고 생각했어.(sick in bed)

_____

나는 네가 아파서 침대에 있어 왔다고 생각했어.　_____

Pattern 4_ 과학적 사실, 속담, 반복적 행위, 직업일 경우 항상 현재시제

소년은 빛이 소리보다 빠르다는 것을 배웠다.(travel)_____

Brian은 항상 아침에 운동한다고 말했다.　_____

Pattern 5_ 역사적인 사실의 경우 항상 과거시제

우리는 시저가 로마제국의 첫 번째 황제였다는 것을 안다.(Caesar, the first Roman emperor)

_____

Pattern 6_ 시간과 조건을 나타내는 부사절은 현재시제가 미래 대신

동생이 집에 돌아오면, 나는 그를 꽉 안아 줄 거야.(~give him a big hug)

_____

Unit

71_ 화법

● **Pattern** 주어＋said "주어＋동사" (직접화법)

→ 주어＋said that 주어＋동사 (간접화법)

(At the party)

A: Hey, Judy! I'm glad you are here. I thought you said you couldn't come.

B: Yes, I did. But the meeting was *put off.

A: Good. Come and sit here. Would you care for a drink?

B: Yes, I'd like some orange juice.

*put off 연기하다

---

1. 화법

다른 사람의 말을 전달하는 표현방법을 화법이라고 하는데, 화법에는 다른 사람의 말을 그대로 전달하는 직접화법이 있고, 다른 사람의 말을 전달하는 사람 입장에서 고쳐 말하는 간접화법이 있다.

직접화법	간접화법
He <u>says,</u> "<u>I'm bored</u>" 전달동사　피전달문	He says that <u>he is bored.</u> 피전달문
전달 동사 다음에 콤마(,)를 찍고 피전달문에는 따옴표(" ")를 쓴다.	피전달문의 따옴표(" ")를 없애고 말을 전달하는 사람 입장으로 바꿔 표현한다.

2. 평서문(피전달문)의 화법전환

> ● 방법
>
> 1. 콤마(,)와 따옴표(" ") 삭제
>
> 2. 전달동사 say → say, say to → tell
>
> 3. 접속사 that을 쓴다.
>
> 4. 인칭대명사와 부사를 적절하게 바꾸고 시제를 일치시킨다.

Nick **said, "I have to go now."** Nick은 "나는 지금 가야 돼"라고 말했다.

→ Nick **said (that) he had to go then.** Nick은 그때 가야한다고 말했다.

→ Nick **told me (that) he had to go then.** Nick은 내게 그때 가야한다고 말했다.

*말을 듣는 사람을 밝히고 싶으면 「tell＋사람」을 쓴다.

Jack **said to me, "Your brother didn't come here."** Jack은 "네 남동생이 여기에 오지 않았어."라고 말했다.

→Jack **told me that my brother hadn't gone there.** Jack이 내 남동생이 거기에 가지 않았다고 말했다.

146

now → then	today → that day	tomorrow → the next day
yesterday → the day before	tonight → that night	last night → the night before
ago → before	this(these) → that(those)	here → there

4. 의문문(피전달문)의 화법전환

> ● 방법
>
> 1. 콤마(,)와 따옴표(" ") 삭제
>
> 2. 전달동사 say/ say to/ ask → ask
>
> 3. 피전달문은 의문사가 있는 경우 간접의문문형태인 「의문사 + 주어 + 동사」로 바꿔준다. 의문사가 없는 경우 「whether/ if(~인지 아닌지) + 주어 + 동사」형태를 쓴다.
>
> 4. 인칭대명사와 부사를 적절하게 바꾸고 시제를 일치시킨다.

I **said to the boy, "Where do you live?"** 나는 소년에게 말했다. "어디에 사니?"
→ I **asked the boy where he lived.** 나는 소년에게 그가 어디에 사는 지 물었다.

I **asked the police officer, "How far is it?"** 나는 경찰에게 물었다, "얼마나 멀어요?"
→ I **asked the police officer how far it was.** 나는 경찰에게 얼마나 먼지 물었다.

David **said, "Is this your car?"** David은 말했다. "이게 네 차니?"
→ David **asked whether(=if) that was my car.** David은 이게 내 차인지 물었다.

The girl **said to me, "Have you ever seen a wizard?"** 그 소녀가 내게 말했다. "마법사를 본적 있어요?"
→ The girl **asked whether(=if) I had seen a wizard.** 그 소녀가 내게 마법사를 본적 있는 지 물었다.

5. 명령문(피전달문)의 화법전환

> ● 방법: 전달문의 전달동사를 문맥에 맞추어 tell(지시), ask(요청), command/ order(명령), advise(충고), invite(초대) 등으로 바꿔주고 목적어 뒤에 「to + 동사원형」을 쓴다. 그리고 대명사와 부사를 적절하게 바꾼다.
>
> 「주어 + say (to + 목적어), "명령문"」 → 「주어 + 동사(tell/ask/order/advise~) + 목적어 + to 부정사」

My mother **said to me, "Put away your books."** 엄마가 내게 "네 책들 치워."라고 말씀하셨다.
→ My mother **told me to put away my books.** 엄마가 내 책을 치우라고 말씀하셨다.

Henry **said to me, "Would you like to go out with me?"** Henry가 내게 "데이트할래?"라고 말했다.
→ Henry **asked me to go out with him.** Henry가 내게 데이트하자고 (요청)했다.

Unit Test

1. 직접화법 문장을 간접화법 문장으로 바꾸시오.

1. Laura said, "I don't like vegetables."

→ _____

2. David said, "I'm really hungry."

→ _____

3. Tom said, "I woke up feeling sick, so I stayed in bed."

→ _____

4. Nick said to me, "I have to go now."

→ _____

5. I said to the girl, "Where do you live?"

→ _____

6. David asked, "Is this your bag?"

→ _____

7. My boss said, "Finish your report by tomorrow."

→ _____

8. Captain Kim said to private Lee, "Don't move."

→ _____

2. 다음 대화를 보고 보기와 같이 상대방과 반대의견을 써 보시오.

> 보기 │ A: Tom is coming to the party.
>   B: He is? I thought you said <u>he wasn't coming to the party.</u>

1. A: I'm going out tonight.

   B: You are? I thought you said _____

2. A: English is difficult.

   B: It is? I thought you said _____

3. A: I'm leaving for Tokyo.

   B: You are. I thought you said _____

4. A: That restaurant is expensive.

   B: It is? I thought you said _____

5. A: David likes me.

   B: He does? I thought you said _____

Writing Pattern Practice | 화법

Pattern 1_ 평서문(피전달문)의 화법전환(직접화법 → 간접화법)

Nick은 "나는 지금 가야 돼"라고 말했다.
(Nick said, "I have to go now.")   → _____

Jack은 "네 남동생이 여기에 오지 않았어."라고 말했다.
(Jack said to me, "Your brother didn't come here.")

                                   → _____

Pattern 2_ 의문문(피전달문)의 화법전환(직접화법 → 간접화법)

나는 소녀에게 말했다. "무엇을 먹고 있니?"
(I said to the girl, "What are you eating?")   → _____

나는 경찰에게 물었다, "어디가 가장 가까운 은행이에요?"
(I asked the police officer, "Where is the nearest bank?")

                                   → _____

David은 말했다. "이게 네 펜이니?"
(David said, "Is this your pen?")   → _____

그 소년이 내게 말했다. "공룡 본 적 있어요?"
(The boy said to me, "Have you ever seen a dinosaur?")

                                   → _____

Pattern 3_ 명령문(피전달문)의 화법전환(직접화법 → 간접화법)

엄마가 내게 "네 방을 치워."라고 말씀하셨다.
(My mother said to me, "Clean your room.")   → _____

Sam이 내게 "내 생일파티에 올래?"라고 말했다.
(Sam said to me, "Will you come to my birthday party?")(invite)

                                   → _____

Vicky가 내게 "창문 좀 닫아줄래?"라고 말했다.
(Vicky said to me, "Please close the window.")(ask)

                                   → _____

Unit

72 강조, 도치

● Pattern   강조: do+동사원형
의문사+on earth/ in the world+~
It is/was ~that

A: **There goes David and Ann.**
B: **I don't understand why David goes out with Ann.**
A: Neither do I. **She is such *a know-it-all and talks as if she knew everything.**
B: **What do you think David sees in her?**   *a know-it-all 뭐든지 아는 척하는 사람

---

1. 동사 강조

동사의 의미를 강조하는 경우 조동사 do를 쓰며 '정말 ~하다'로 해석한다. 이때 do의 시제는 본동사의 원래 시제를 취하며 동사는 동사원형을 쓴다.

I love you. → I **do** love you. 나는 정말 너를 사랑해.
Brian likes English. → Brian **does** like English. Brian은 정말 영어를 좋아해.
I sent the present to Jerry. → I **did** send the present to Jerry. 내가 Jerry에게 정말 선물을 보냈는데.

2. 의문문 강조

의문문에 on earth, in the world 등을 사용하면 '도대체'라는 의미가 추가된다. 위치는 대부분 의문사 다음에 온다.

What **on earth** are you doing? 너는 도대체 무엇을 하고 있니?
Who **in the world** stole the money? 누가 도대체 그 돈을 훔쳤을까?

3. It is/was ~ that 강조

I saw Heather in the park yesterday. 나는 어제 공원에서 Heather을 봤다.

● 주어강조
It was **I** that(=who) saw Heather in the park yesterday. 어제 Heather을 공원에서 본 사람은 나였다.

● 목적어강조
It was **Heather** that(=whom) I saw in the park yesterday. 어제 내가 공원에서 본 사람은 Heather였다.

● 부사(장소)강조
It was **in the park** that(=where) I saw Heather yesterday. 내가 어제 Heather을 본 곳은 공원이었다.

● 부사(시간)강조
It was **yesterday** that(=when) I saw Heather in the park 내가 Heather을 공원에서 본 것은 어제였다.

150

4. 장소 부사어 강조를 위한 도치

부사(구)를 문장 맨 앞에 위치시킨다. 주어/동사의 위치는 상황에 따라 다를 수 있음을 유의한다.

> 「주어＋동사＋here/there」
>
> → 「Here/There＋동사＋명사주어」 또는 「Here/There＋대명사주어＋동사」

Your sister comes here. → **Here** comes your sister. 여기 네 여동생 오네.
The bus goes there. → **There** goes the bus. 저기 버스 가네.

I MORE TIPS I here/there가 문두로 와서 강조되는 그 밖의 경우
• **Here/There** you are.(＝Here/There you go.) 여기 있어.(무엇을 건네줄 때)
• **Here** we are. 다 왔다.(도착했을 때)
• **Here/There** it is. 그것이 여기/거기 있었구나.(무엇/누군가를 발견했을 때)

5. 부정어 강조를 위한 도치

> 「부정부사어구＋be동사/조동사＋주어」
>
> *부정 부사어구에는 not, never, hardly, scarcely, seldom, rarely, not only, not until(~해서야…하다) 등이 있다

I have never been this disappointed.
→ **Never have I been** this disappointed. 지금까지 이렇게 실망해 본 적이 없다.
He had rarely seen such a sunset.
→ **Rarely had he seen** such a sunset. 그는 그런 일몰을 거의 보지 못했었다.
I couldn't sleep until my mother came back home.
→ **Not until** my mother came back home **could I sleep.** 엄마가 집에 돌아오신 후에야 잠들 수 있었다.
Jenny is not only pretty, but she is so kind to everybody.
→ **Not only** is Jenny pretty, but she is so kind to everybody. Jenny는 예쁠 뿐 아니라 모두에게 친절하다.

*부정어 강조를 위한 도치는 일상회화보다 문학작품 등에서 볼 수 있다.

6. so, neither 다음의 도치

앞에서 한 말에 대해 '~도 또한 그러하다'는 의미로 긍정문 뒤에는 「So+동사+주어」를, 부정문 뒤에는 「Neither+동사+주어」를 쓴다.

> 앞 문장: 일반동사 → 「So/Neither＋do/does/did＋주어」
>
> 앞 문장: be동사 → 「So/Neither＋be동사＋주어」
>
> 앞 문장: 조동사 → 「So/Neither＋조동사＋주어」

A: I like jazz. B: **So do I.**(=I like jazz, too) A: 나는 재즈를 좋아해. B: 나도 그래.
A: I can't eat any more. B: **Neither can I.**(=I can't eat any more, either.)
A: 나는 더 이상 못 먹겠어. B: 나도 그래.

Unit Test

1. 다음 문장을 괄호안의 지시에 따라 강조문장으로 바꿔 쓰시오.

1. He lied to me. (do를 이용한 동사 강조)

→ _____

2. What are you talking about? (on earth를 이용한 의문문 강조)

→ _____

3. Who broke into the house? (in the world를 이용한 의문문 강조)

→ _____

4. I met Kate at the cafe. (It~that을 이용한 주어 강조)

→ _____

5. I met Kate at the cafe. (It~that을 이용한 목적어 강조)

→ _____

6. I met Kate at the cafe. (It~that을 이용한 부사구 강조)

→ _____

2. 다음 문장을 괄호안의 지시에 따라 도치문장으로 바꿔 쓰시오.

1. Your mother comes here. (장소부사어 강조를 위한 도치)

→ _____

2. The taxi goes there. (장소부사어 강조를 위한 도치)

→ _____

3. It goes there. (장소부사어 강조를 위한 도치)

→ _____

4. I have never seen a ghost. (부정어 강조를 위한 도치)

→ _____

3. 다음 주어진 문장에 So~ 또는 Neither~을 사용하여 동의하는 문장을 쓰시오.

1. A: I get paid monthly.
   B: _____
2. A: I can't stand loud noises.
   B: _____
3. A: I'm tired of doing the same things all the time.
   B: _____
4. A: I haven't been to Europe.
   B: _____
5. A: I must stop smoking.
   B: _____

Writing Pattern Practice | 강조, 도치

Pattern 1_ 「do/does/did + 동사원형」 동사강조

나는 정말 너를 사랑해. _____

John은 정말 스포츠를 싫어해. _____

그는 정말 회의에 참석했어. _____

Pattern 2_ 「의문사 + on earth/ in the world + 동사원형」 의문문 강조

너는 도대체 어디에 가고 있니? _____

누가 도대체 그 돈을 훔쳤을까? _____

Pattern 3_ 「It + is/was + 강조할 단어/구 + that」을 이용한 강조

내가 그를 본 것은 어제였다. _____

내가 원하는 것은 커피다. _____

내가 사랑하는 사람은 네가 아니다. _____

내가 본 것은 Judy가 아니었다. _____

내가 그녀를 만난 곳은 독일에서가 아니었다. _____

Pattern 4_ 「Here/There + 동사 + 명사주어」 또는 「Here/There +대명사주어 + 동사」 장소 부사어 강조를 위한 도치

여기 네 여동생 오네. _____

저기 버스 가네. _____

여기 그녀가 오네. _____

저기 그것이 가네. _____

Pattern 5_ 「부정부사어구 + be동사/조동사 + 주어」 부정어 강조를 위한 도치

지금까지 이렇게 긴장해 본 적이 없다.(Never have~, nervous)

_____

Pattern 6_ 「So/Neither + do/does/did + 주어」, 「So/Neither + be동사 + 주어」, 「So/Neither + 조동사 + 주어」

A: I'm hungry. B: 나도 그래. _____

A: I was late to school. B: 나도 그래. _____

A: I haven't tried Thai food. B: 나도 그래. _____

73_ 생략

● Pattern   생략 : 반복어구 생략
          부사절에서 「주어＋동사」 생략
          관용어구 생략

A: I'd like to use your car if possible.
B: Well, until when?
A: Until the end of the month.
B: I'm not sure. I'll have to think about it.

1. 생략

영어에서는 간결성이 매우 중요하다. 그러므로 반복되거나 없어도 미루어 짐작할 수 있는 말은 생략되는 경우가 많다. 특히 내용을 짧게 압축해서 표현해야 하는 광고문, 신문의 헤드라인, 안내판, 격언 등에서 흔히 생략되는 경우가 많다.

2. 중복을 피하기 위한 생략

I met George and **(I)** had dinner with him. 나는 George를 만나서 (나는) 그와 저녁을 먹었다.
I don't sing as well as you **(sing)**. 나는 너 만큼(네가 노래 부르는 것만큼) 노래 못한다.
He wanted to go but he wasn't able *<u>to **(go)**</u>. 그는 가기를 원했지만 그럴 수 없었다.

*대부정사: 반복을 피하기 위해 to부정사에서 to만으로 앞의 동사를 대신함

3. 부사절에서 「주어 + 동사」 생략

when, before, though, if, unless 등의 시간, 양보, 조건 등의 접속사가 사용된 부사절에서는 「주어＋동사」가 생략되는 경우가 있다.
I'll give you the money today **if (it is) necessary.** 필요하면 내가 오늘 그 돈을 줄게.
I'd like to borrow this book **if (it is) possible.** 가능하면 이 책을 빌리고 싶어.
Though (he is) rich, he's not happy at all. 부자지만 그는 전혀 행복하지 않다.

4. 관용어구

No smoking! 수영금지 (=No smoking is allowed.)
No parking! 주차금지 (=No parking is allowed.)
No pains, no gains! 수고 없이 소득은 없다.(=If you take no pains, you will get no gains.)
Hands off! 손대지 마시오.(=Keep your hands off this.)
First come, first served. 선착순입니다.(=If you come first, you will be served first.)

Unit Test

1. 보기와 같이 빈칸에 생략된 말을 알맞게 쓰시오.

> 보기 | I met John and <u>I</u> had dinner with him.
>   If <u>it is</u> necessary, I'll give them a ride.

1. A: I think Elvis was the best singer ever.
   B: Yes, he was _____.
2. Though _____ sick, he did his best on the exam.
3. I'd like to borrow this book if _____ possible.
4. I don't speak English as well as you _____.
5. When _____ young, she was very pretty.

2. 보기와 같이 주어진 말을 '주어+동사'가 있는 완벽한 문장으로 바꿔 쓰려고 한다. 빈칸에 알맞은 말을 써 넣으시오.

> 보기 | No smoking! → No smoking is allowed.
>   Sorry! → I am sorry.

1. No soliciting!   *잡상인금지
→ No soliciting _____ _____.
2. Glad to meet you!
→ _____ _____ glad to meet you.
3. First come, first served.
→ If you come first, you'll be _____ _____.

3. 보기와 같이 다음 문장에서 불필요한 말을 생략하려고 한다. 빈칸에 알맞은 말을 써 넣으시오.

> 보기 | No swimming is allowed. → No swimming!
>   I wish you a good morning. → Good morning!

1. I'll see you later.
_____ _____ _____!

2. If you take no pains, you will get no gains.
_____ _____ _____ _____!

3. Keep your hands off this.
_____ _____!

Writing Pattern Practice | 생략

Pattern 1_ 반복어구 생략

나는 George를 만나서 (나는) 그와 저녁을 먹었다. _____

A: Was he at the meeting? B: 응, 그는 그랬어(회의에 왔었어).

_____

나는 너 (네가 부르는) 만큼 노래 못한다.(I don't~) _____

Did you feed the dog? 아니, 하지만 하려고(먹이주려고).(be going to)

_____

그냥 내가 (하라고) 말한 대로 해.(as, tell) _____

Pattern 2_ 부사절에서 「주어 + 동사」 생략

필요하면 내가 오늘 너에게 그 돈을 줄게.(~ if necessary)

_____

가능하면 이 책을 빌리고 싶어.(I'd like) _____

부자지만 그는 전혀 행복하지 않다.(Though~) _____

Pattern 3_ 관용어구

수영금지(No swimming is allowed.) _____

주차금지(No parking is allowed.) _____

수고 없이 소득은 없다.(If you take no pains, you will get no gains.)

_____

손대지 마시오.(Keep your hands off this.) _____

선착순입니다.(If you come first, you will be served first.)

_____

Unit 74 부정표현

● Pattern   few, little
hardly, scarcely, barely, rarely, seldom
「not + all, every, always, both, necessarily, fully, completely등」

Grammar in Practice

A: How's Jess? Are you still seeing him?
B: No, we broke up.
A: How come?
B: We have few things in common. I don't know why I *crushed on him at the first time.

*crush on ~에게 반하다

Grammar in Use

1. 부정의미 형용사

● few: 셀 수 있는 명사 앞에서 '거의 없는'의 뜻으로 쓴다.
There were few passengers in the bus. 버스에는 승객이 거의 없었다.
● little: 셀 수 없는 명사 앞에서 '거의 없는'의 뜻으로 쓴다.
We had very little snow last year. 작년에는 눈이 거의 안 왔다.

2. 부정의미 부사

● hardly, scarcely, barely: '거의 ~하지 않는'
He hardly ever smiles. 그는 좀처럼 웃지 않는다.
I can barely hear you. 네 소리가 거의 안 들려.
● rarely, seldom: '거의 ~한 적이 없는'
Books are seldom returned to their right place on the shelves. 책을 책꽂이의 원래 위치에 되돌려 둔 적이 거의 없다.

3. 부분부정

부분부정은 「not + all, every, always, both, necessarily, fully, completely 등」의 형태로 '항상/ 둘 다/ 반드시/ 완전히 ~한 것은 아니다'라는 뜻이다.
I didn't completely understand what he was saying. 나는 그가 말하는 것을 완전히 이해하지는 못했다.

4. 자주 쓰이는 부정 구문

● Age is **nothing but** a number. '단지 ~인' 나이는 단지 숫자이다.
● He **didn't** stop walking **until** it got dark. '~할 때까지 …하지 않다' 그는 어두워질 때까지 걸음을 멈추지 않았다.
● This ring is **no longer** any meaning to me. '더 이상 ~아니다' 이 반지는 더 이상 나에게 아무 의미도 아니다.

Unit Test

1. 두 문장이 같은 뜻이 되도록 빈칸에 알맞은 말을 보기에서 골라 써 넣으시오.

보기 | not ~ until   completely   rarely   nothing but   no longer

1. I seldom visit my grandparents.
→ I _____ visit my grandparents.
2. I don't fully understand what he is talking about.
→ I don't _____ understand what he is talking about.
3. I'm not any longer interested in him
→ I'm _____ interested in him.
4. He is only a thief.
→ He is _____ a thief.
5. People know the blessing of health when they lose it.
→ People do _____ know the blessing of health _____ they lose it.

2. 우리말과 일치하도록 괄호 안의 단어를 알맞게 배열하시오.

1. 선인장은 물이 거의 필요없다. (cactuses/ little water/ need)

_____

2. Nancy는 coffee를 거의 마시지 않는다. (drinks/ Nancy/ little coffee)

_____

3. 사람들이 거의 그의 생각들을 이해 못한다. (few people/ his ideas/ understand)

_____

4. 그 병에 물이 거의 없다. (little water/ in that bottle/ there is)

_____

5. 나는 그것을 거의 볼 수 없다. (hardly/ I can/ see it)

_____

6. 그가 누군지 잘 모르겠다. (who he is/ I can/ scarcely recognize)

_____

7. 부자라고 항상 행복한 것은 아니다. (the rich/ always happy/ are not)

_____

8. 그녀는 울기만 했다. (cry/ she did/ nothing but)

_____

9. Cindy는 이 도시에 더 이상 머무르고 있지 않다. (no longer/ staying/ Cindy is/ in this city)

_____

10. 그는 엄마가 화를 낼 때까지 TV를 봤다. (stop watching TV/ he didn't/ until his mother got angry)

_____

Writing Pattern Practice | 부정표현

Pattern 1_ 「few, little + 셀 수 있는, 셀 수 없는 명사」 부정의미 형용사

버스에는 승객이 거의 없었다.(~in the bus.)

작년에는 눈이 거의 안 왔다.(We~, very little)

Pattern 2_ 「hardly, scarcely, barely ~」 '거의 ~하지 않는' 부정의미 부사
　　　　　　「rarely, seldom ~」 '거의 ~한 적이 없는'

그는 좀처럼 웃지 않는다.(hardly)

나는 네 소리가 거의 안 들려.(barely, you)

어머니는 다른 사람들 험담을 거의 안하신다.(rarely, ~speaks ill of others)

Pattern 3_ 「not + all, every, always, both, necessarily, fully, completely 등」 부분부정

부자들이라고 항상 행복한 것은 아니다.

Heather가 항상 우리에게 친절한 것은 아니다.

당신 둘 다 기회를 얻을 수 있는 것은 아니다.(Not~ ,get)

나는 그가 말하는 것을 완전히 이해하지는 못했다.(completely, what he was saying)

Pattern 4_ 「nothing but, not ~ until…, no longer」 자주 쓰이는 부정 구문

나이는 단지 숫자이다.

그는 어두워질 때까지 걸음을 멈추지 않았다.(get)

이 반지는 더 이상 나에게 아무 의미도 아니다.(no longer, any meaning)

75 1형식, 2형식, 3형식

- **Pattern**
  1형식 「주어＋동사」
  2형식 「주어＋동사＋보어」
  3형식 「주어＋동사＋목적어」

A: You look really sharp in that suit!

B: Thanks. That dress looks great on you as well.

A: Well, thanks. I was a bit worried this might be too loud.

B: Not at all. Don't worry.

---

1. 문장의 형식

영어의 모든 문장은 목적어나 보어의 필요유무에 따라 5가지 형식으로 분류한다. 이 때 부사(구) 등의 수식어는 형식에 영향을 미치지 않는다. 문장형식의 이해는 긴 문장의 구조를 빠르고 정확하게 분석하는것과, 문장을 의미단위로 나누어 직독직해 하는 능력을 키우는데 큰 도움이 될 것이다.

<u>My uncle</u> <u>in New York</u> <u>works</u> <u>at a bank.</u> 뉴욕에 있는 삼촌은 은행에서 일하신다.
　주어　　 형용사구　　 동사　　 부사구

→ 1형식 문장

2. 1형식 문형

「주어＋동사」만으로 완전한 의미를 나타낼 수 있으며, 수식어구인 형용사구나 부사구 등이 붙기도 한다.

- '～가 …하다'

go(가다), come(오다), fly, smile, appear, fall, lie(눕다), die, happen, do(적당하다), count(중요하다) 등

A nice convertible suddenly **appeared** when I walked down the street. 길을 걷는데 멋진 오픈카가 갑자기 나타났다.

- '～가 …되다' *해석에 주의해야 할 동사들이다.

open(열리다), close(닫히다), increase(증가되다), stop(멈추다), sell(팔리다), do(도움이 되다, 충분하다), work(작동되다, 효과있다) 등

The population continues to **increase**. 인구는 지속적으로 증가된다.
Will this **do**? 이거면 될까요?

- '～가 …에 있다'

대부분 「There＋be동사(＋장소 전치사구)」 형식으로 나타낸다.

There are several cars parked on the street. 거리에는 차가 여러 대 주차되어 있다.

3. 2형식 문형

「주어＋동사＋보어」 형태로 동사만으로는 주어에 대한 설명이 부족해, 주어의 상태나 동작을 설명하는 주격보어를 필요로 하는 문형이다. 주격보어가 될 수 있는 것은 명사, 형용사 등이다.

2형식에 주로 쓰이는 동사			
look ~하게 보이다 smell ~의 냄새가 나다 taste ~의 맛이 나다 sound ~하게 들리다 feel ~하게 느껴지다	become ~되다 get ~되다 turn ~되다 grow ~되다 go ~되다(주로 나쁜 쪽으로)	turn out ~로 판명되다 come out~가 드러나다	remain ~대로이다 keep 계속~인 채로 있다 stay 계속~인 채로 있다

Do I **sound** <u>strange</u> today? 오늘 내 목소리 이상해?
　　　　　　보어:형용사

The argument **remained** <u>unresolved.</u> 논쟁은 해결되지 않았다.
　　　　　　　　　　보어:형용사

The only thing that matters **is** <u>to find our way there.</u> 오직 중요한 것은 거기에 가는
　　　　　　　　　　　　　　　보어: 명사구
길을 찾는 것이다.

The problem **is** <u>that you don't have enough money to study abroad.</u> 문제는
네가 유학 갈 충분한 돈이 없는 것이다.　　　　　　　　　　보어:명사절

4. 3형식 문형

「주어＋동사＋목적어」 형태로 동사가 나타내는 행위의 대상이 있는 경우에 쓰는 문형이다. 목적어 자리에는 명사, 대명사, 부정사, 동명사 등이 올 수 있다.

Most people **drink** too much <u>soda.</u> 대부분의 사람들은 너무 많은 탄산음료를 마신다.
　　　　　　　　　　　목적어:명사

Who **owns** <u>the car</u> which is parked outside? 밖에 주차되어 있는 차는 누구 거니?
　　　　　목적어:명사

We don't **allow** <u>smoking</u> in the lecture room. 우리는 강의실에서 흡연을 허락하지 않는다.
　　　　　　　목적어:동명사

I **wonder** <u>who to invite.</u> 누구를 초대해야 할 지 의문이다.
　　　　　목적어:명사구

I **understood** <u>the importance of our being there.</u> 나는 우리가 거기에 가는 것에 대한 중
요성을 알고 있었다.　　　　목적어:명사구

I **feel sorry** <u>that I lost my temper</u> this morning. 아침에 화내서 미안해.
　　　　　　목적어:명사절

I **wonder** <u>if you could lend me some money.</u> 나는 네가 돈을 좀 빌려줄 수 있는지 궁금해.
　　　　　　　목적어:명사절

I **want to know** <u>why he told me a lie.</u> 나는 그가 왜 거짓말을 했는지 알고 싶다.
　　　　　　　목적어:명사절

Unit Test

1. 다음 문장의 형식을 쓰시오.

    1. I write to my mother once a month. (   )

    2. The truth is that he didn't steal the necklace. (   )

    3. I understood he was honest. (   )

    4. I insisted that she should see the doctor at once. (   )

    5. You look just like your mother. (   )

    6. A black cat suddenly appeared in front of me. (   )

    7. I thought you were in Thailand. (   )

    8. There is a lot of noise in the street. (   )

    9. Something smells really bad. (   )

    10. Once upon a time there were three wicked brothers. (   )

    11. I hope that you will have a wonderful time. (   )

    12. There must be somebody at home. (   )

    13. I'll become a musician. (   )

    14. The point is that she's not attractive. (   )

    15. There was a boy water-skiing on the lake. (   )

2. 문장의 주격보어에 동그라미 하시오.

    1. The wine tastes funny.

    2. You look gorgeous today.

    3. This is what I wanted.

    4. Your dream will come true.

    5. The important thing is to find the way to the station.

    6. The problem is that you have no money.

    7. The truth is that Jane is going out with Nick.

3. 문장의 목적어에 동그라미 하시오.

    1. Do you enjoy working?

    2. I love to go for a walk.

    3. I don't know what to buy for Cindy.

    4. I don't think it will rain.

    5. They thought that she was fascinating.

    6. I was wondering if I could do anything to help.

    7. I didn't understand what you were trying to say.

Writing Pattern Practice | 1형식, 2형식, 3형식

Pattern 1_ 「주어 + 동사」 1형식

나는 어머니께 한 달에 한번 편지를 쓴다.(write to) _____

내가 길을 걸을 때 멋진 오픈카가 갑자기 나타났다.(A nice convertible~, walk down the street)

_____

은행에 사람이 많이 있다.(a lot of) _____

우리 사이에 오해가 좀 있다.(~between us) _____

네가 알아야 할 무엇인가가 있다.(~you have to know)

_____

Pattern 2_ 「주어 + 동사 + 보어」 2형식

오늘 내 목소리 이상해?(sound) _____

문제는 네가 유학 갈 충분한 돈이 없는 것이다.(study abroad)

_____

사실은 나는 그것에 대해 아무것도 모른다.(The fact~, nothing)

_____

Pattern 3_ 「주어 + 동사 + 목적어」 3형식

대부분의 사람들은 너무 많은 탄산음료를 마신다.(~too much soda)

_____

밖에 주차되어 있는 차는 누구 거니?(Who owns~, which is)

_____

우리는 강의실에서 흡연을 허락하지 않는다.(~in the lecture room)

_____

나는 누구를 초대해야 할 지 의문이다.(I wonder~) _____

아침에 화를 내서 미안해.(I feel~, lose my temper)

_____

나는 네가 돈을 좀 빌려줄 수 있는지 궁금해.(I wonder~, could)

_____

나는 그가 내게 왜 거짓말을 했는지 알고 싶다.(I want to~)

_____

76_ 4형식, 5형식

● **Pattern** 4형식 「주어＋동사＋간접목적어＋직접목적어」
5형식 「주어＋동사＋목적보어」

A: Why do you look so sad? Something wrong?
B: I'm just sick of working with people who are too *conceited.
A: That makes two of us. I find people who always show off *irritating.
B: I think so.

*conceited 우쭐대는 *irritating 짜증나는

1. 4형식

「주어 ＋ 동사 ＋ 간접목적어 ＋ 직접목적어」형태로 목적어를 두개 필요로 한다. 목적어 중 먼저 나와서 '～에게' 라고 해석되는 목적어를 「간접목적어」라고 하며, 그 뒤에 오는 '～을(를)' 이라고 해석하는 목적어를 「직접목적어」라고 한다. teach, send, tell, lend, show, buy, make, write, ask, offer, pay 등의 동사가 4형식에 주로 쓰인다.

He **showed** <u>me</u> <u>the way</u> to the mall. 그가 내게 mall에 가는 길을 알려줬다.
　　　　　　간접목적어 직접목적어

2. 4형식↔3형식

● give, show, tell, offer 등을 포함한 대부분 4형식 문장은 「주어 ＋ 동사 ＋ 직접목적어 ＋ to ＋ 간접목적어」(3형식)로 바꿀 수 있다.
The waiter **offered** him red wine. 웨이터는 그에게 레드와인을 제공했다.
→ He offered red wine **to** him.

● buy, get, make, find, choose 등의 동사가 쓰인 4형식 문장은 「주어 ＋ 동사 ＋ 직접목적어 ＋ for ＋ 간접목적어」(3형식)의 형태로 바꿀 수 있다.
Please **get** me something to write with. 내게 쓸 것(필기도구)을 가져와.
→ Please get something to write with **for** me.
Will you **find** me a good one? 내게 좋은 것을 찾아줄래?
→ Will you find a good one **for** me?

| **MORE TIPS** | 우리말로 할 때는 '～을…에게' 라는 의미로 번역되어 마치 4형식동사처럼 생각되지만 실제로는 3형식동사인 경우들이 있다. 아래 예문에서 전치사가 빠지면 틀린 문장이 된다. 시험에 자주 출제되는 문법사항이다.
David **announced to** us his plan. David은 우리에게 그의 계획을 발표했다.
I **confessed to** Mary that I had taken her watch. 나는 Mary에게 시계를 가져갔다고 고백했다.
I will **explain to** you what this means. 내가 이것이 무슨 의미인지 네게 설명할게.
They **imposed** a tax of 1000 dollars **on** me. 그들은 내게 1000달러의 세금과 부과했다.

3. 5형식

「주어 + 동사 + 목적어 + 목적격보어」 형태로 목적어와 보어관계는 의미상 주어와 술어 관계이다. 목적보어 자리에는 명사나 형용사, 또는 준동사(부정사, 원형부정사) 등이 올 수 있다.

● 보어가 명사일 경우 「주어 + make, call, name 등 + 목적어 + 명사」

We **call** him <u>Mr. Perfect.</u> 우리는 그를 완벽주의자라고 부른다.

● 보어가 형용사일 경우 「주어 + make, keep, suppose, would like, want, push 등 + 목적어 + 형용사」

What **makes** you so <u>depressed?</u> 뭐 때문에 그렇게 우울하니?

Most people **supposed** him <u>guilty.</u> 대부분의 사람들은 그가 유죄라고 생각했다.

I**'d like** my eggs <u>scrambled.</u> 달걀을 스크램블해 주세요.

I **want** my hair <u>cut.</u> 머리를 자르고 싶어요.

She **pushed** the door <u>shut.</u> 그녀는 문을 밀어서 닫았다.

● 보어가 to부정사일 경우 「주어 + tell, want, would like, allow, expect + 목적어 + to부정사」

How many times do I have to **tell** you not <u>to be</u> late? 몇 번이나 늦지 말라고 말해야하니?

I **want** you <u>to fill</u> out the form. 나는 네가 양식에 기입했으면 좋겠어.

Would you **like** me <u>to go</u> back home? 너는 내가 집에 돌아갔으면 좋겠니?

They don't **allow** us <u>to smoke</u> in this building. 그들은 이 빌딩에서 담배 피도록 허락하지 않는다.

● 보어가 원형부정사일 경우 「주어 + see, watch, hear, feel, make, have, let 등 + 목적어 + 원형부정사」

I like **watching** my children <u>sing.</u> 나는 내 아이들이 노래하는 것을 지켜보는 것이 좋다.

I want to **make** my girlfriend <u>feel</u> happy today. 나는 오늘 여자친구를 행복하게 만들어주고 싶어.

Let me <u>know</u> if something important comes up. 중요한 일이 생기면 알려줘.

Unit Test

1. 다음 문장의 형식을 쓰시오.

1. His father left him a large fortune. (   )
2. Push the door open. (   )
3. The cold weather had already turned the leaves red and yellow. (   )
4. She kept me waiting so long. (   )
5. Do not leave the door open. (   )
6. I will make you a new suit. (   )
7. Most people supposed him guilty. (   )
8. What makes you so tired? (   )
9. I'd like my eggs scrambled. (   )
10. He showed me the way to the mall. (   )
11. How many times do I have to tell you not to be late? (   )
12. Get Tom something to drink. (   )
13. I will make you spaghetti for lunch. (   )
14. Each girl kept her love a secret. (   )
15. Did he lend you the money? (   )
16. Helen brought me some beautiful roses from her garden. (   )

2. 틀린 곳을 찾아 밑줄치고 고쳐 쓰시오.

1. Could you buy a nice motorbike to me?   → _____
2. Give that book back for your brother.   → _____
3. Would you like me do this for you?   → _____
4. I'd like my hair cutting.   → _____
5. I want to make my girlfriend felt special today. → _____

3. 우리말과 일치하도록 괄호 안의 단어를 알맞게 배열하시오.

1. 뭐 때문에 그렇게 행복하니? (makes/ what/ you/ so happy/ ?)

_____

2. 염색해 주세요. (my hair/ I'd like/ dyed)

_____

3. 내가 네게 늦지 말라고 말했잖아. (you/ not to be late/ I/ told)

_____

4. 내가 가기를 원하니? (me/ would you like/ to go/ ?)

_____

5. 누가 문을 열어 두었니? (left the door/ who/ open/ ?)

_____

Writing Pattern Practice | 4형식, 5형식

Pattern 1_ 「주어 + teach, send, tell, lend, show, buy, make, write, ask, offer, pay + 간접목적어 + 직접목적어」 4형식

그가 내게 은행에 가는 길을 알려줬다.(the way) _____

그녀가 내게 부탁을 했다.(a favor) _____

Pattern 2_ 「주어 + give, show, tell, offer 등 + 직접목적어 + to + 간접목적어」 3형식

그는 내게 마실 것을 권했다.(a drink) _____

그것을 내게 돌려줘.(back) _____

Pattern 3_ 「주어 + buy, get, make, find, choose 등 + 직접목적어 + for + 간접목적어」 3형식

내게 좋은 것을 찾아줄래?(Will you~, one) _____

Pattern 4_ 「주어 + make, call, name 등 + 목적어 + 명사」 5형식

너는 나를 네가 원하는 대로 불러도 돼.(You can~, whatever)

_____

누가 네 이름을 Bob이라고 지었니? _____

Pattern 5_ 「주어 + make, keep, suppose, would like, want, push 등 + 목적어 + 형용사」 5형식

뭐 때문에 그렇게 당황해하니?(What~, so embarrassed)

_____

머리를 자르고 싶어요.(I want~) _____

그녀는 문을 밀어서 닫았다. _____

Pattern 6_ 「주어 + tell, want, would like, allow, expect 등 + 목적어 + to부정사」 5형식

몇 번이나 내가 네게 늦지 말라고 말해야하니?(How many times~, have to)

_____

나는 네가 양식에 기입했으면 좋겠어.(want, the form) _____

Pattern 7_ 「주어 + see, watch, hear, feel, make, have, let 등 + 목적어 + 원형부정사」 5형식

나는 오늘 여자친구를 행복하게 만들어주고 싶어. _____

네가 질문 있으면 내게 알려줘.(Let me~) _____

1. 둘 중 알맞은 것을 고르시오.

1. People say that haste (makes/ made) waste.

2. Sally said that she (may/ might) leave for Las Vegas this winter.

3. I always (play/ played) tennis on Saturdays.

4. If I (see/ will see) her, I'll give her your love.

5. I knew you (are/ were) sick in bed.

2. David이 자신에 관해 다음과 같이 말했다. 전달자 입장에서 다시 쓰시오.

> 1. David said, "I'm a college student."
> 2. He said, "I live on my own and work two jobs."
> 3. He said, "I've been always busy making money for two years."
> 4. He said, "I think I can go to Italy to study music next year."

1. David told me that _____

2. He told me that _____

3. He told me that _____

4. He told me that _____

3. 다음 문장을 괄호 안의 지시에 따라 바꿔 쓰시오.

1. I thought I'd pass the test, and <u>I passed</u>. (do를 이용한 밑줄친 문장의 동사강조)

_____

2. She seems to be crying. (do를 이용한 동사강조)

_____

3. Come in. (do를 이용한 동사강조)

_____

4. Where have you been? (on earth를 이용한 의문문 강조)

_____

5. Why did she marry Sam? (in the world를 이용한 의문문 강조)

_____

6. John ate spaghetti for lunch at TGIF's. (It~that을 이용한 주어 강조)

_____

7. John ate spaghetti for lunch at TGIF's. (It~that을 이용한 목적어 강조)

_____

8. John ate spaghetti for lunch at TGIF's. (It~that을 이용한 장소 강조)

_____

9. The bus comes here. (장소부사어 강조를 위한 도치)

_____

10. We have never seen such a good player. (부정어 강조를 위한 도치)

_____

※ ✓표 한 곳에 생략된 알맞은 말을 고르시오.

1. I'll bring a bottle of wine if ✓ necessary.

① I am   ② you are
③ they are   ④ it is

2. She can walk three times faster than I ✓.

① could walk   ② walk
③ can walk   ④ walk fast

3. Though ✓ nice-looking, he is very conceited.

① he is   ② it is
③ he has   ④ he does

※ 다음 문장의 형식을 고르시오.

4. I wonder if she found anything.

① 1형식   ② 2형식
③ 3형식   ④ 4형식
⑤ 5형식

5. My aim is to pass the examination.

① 1형식   ② 2형식
③ 3형식   ④ 4형식
⑤ 5형식

6. I wish you a merry Christmas.

① 1형식   ② 2형식
③ 3형식   ④ 4형식
⑤ 5형식

7. Sue brought me some beautiful roses from her garden.

① 1형식   ② 2형식
③ 3형식   ④ 4형식
⑤ 5형식

8. My uncle in Chicago works for IBM.

① 1형식   ② 2형식
③ 3형식   ④ 4형식
⑤ 5형식

9. Who owns the car which is parked outside?

① 1형식   ② 2형식
③ 3형식   ④ 4형식
⑤ 5형식

10. Who left the door open?

① 1형식   ② 2형식
③ 3형식   ④ 4형식
⑤ 5형식

11. The only thing that I worry about is how I can make that much money.

① 1형식   ② 2형식
③ 3형식   ④ 4형식
⑤ 5형식

12. I find the man who I met at the party irritating.

① 1형식   ② 2형식
③ 3형식   ④ 4형식
⑤ 5형식

13. I don't know where she will be tomorrow.

① 1형식   ② 2형식
③ 3형식   ④ 4형식
⑤ 5형식

14. I believe it true that he canceled the contract.

① 1형식   ② 2형식
③ 3형식   ④ 4형식
⑤ 5형식

REVIEW 2

※ 다음은 친구에게 보내는 이메일이다. 질문에 답하시오.(15~16)

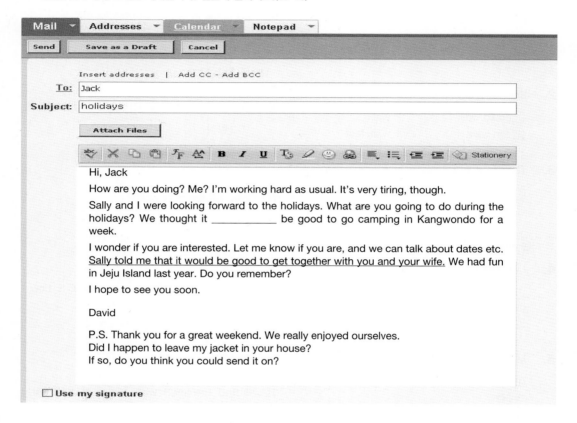

15. 다음 빈칸에 들어갈 말로 가장 적당한 것은?

① may   ② might

③ wil   ④ can

16. 밑줄친 문장을 직접화법으로 바꿔 쓰시오.

Sally said to me, " _____

_____ "

17. 다음 글을 읽고, ⓐ와 ⓑ문장의 형식이 알맞게 연결된 것을 고르시오.

Tomatoes have been regarded as healthy food for a long time. ⓐThere is an important thing you have to know about tomatoes. Doctors recommend eating 10 tablespoons of tomato sauce per week. "Inside the tomato is a chemical called lycopene," says a doctor. "This chemical has a wonderful effect." ⓑHe says, "There are added benefits from eating tomato sauce or paste as opposed to plain tomatoes. It helps you *absorb it better into your *intestinal system."

*absorb 흡수하다 *intestinal 장의

① 1형식 - 3형식   ② 1형식 - 4형식   ③ 3형식 - 1형식   ④ 3형식 - 2형식

SMART
English
Grammar
for Speaking & Writing

머리에 쏙쏙 들어오는

정답 및 해설

MENT*O*RS

SMART
English
Grammar
for Speaking & Writing

2권

정답 및 해설

Chapter 05 | 동사의 변형

Unit 41_ 분사의 역할

P.14

Dialogue

A: 나 이번 여름에 Working Holiday하러 해외로 간다.
B: 와! 재미있겠다.
A: 영어도 배우고 아르바이트 자리도 얻을 거야.
B: 그렇다면, 일석이조네.

Unit test

1.

1. exciting - excited
2. writing - wrote
3. building - built
4. surprising - surprised
5. cutting - cut

2.

1. boring
2. driving
3. cut
4. cut
5. locked
6. jaywalking
7. boring, interesting
8. standing
9. smiling
10. dented

3.

1. sleeping
2. mashed
3. surprising
4. exhausted
5. scrambled
6. dyed
7. leaning
8. mixed
9. weeping
10. broken

Writing Pattern Practice

1.

The water is boiling.
The population of the world is increasing very fast.

2.

English is used in many countries.
My car was towed away.

3.

I've waited for Susie for an hour.
It has been a long time since I saw you.

4.

A rolling stone gathers no moss.
Look at the dented car.

5.

The language spoken in Canada is English.

6.

Sally sat watching TV.
That movie was so disappointing.

7.

I saw Jane standing at the bus stop.
Have you ever heard a canary singing?
I found her running away.
I heard my name called.

Unit 42_ 분사구문

P.18

Dialogue

A: 영어가 전보다 많이 늘었네.
B: 고마워.
A: 보통 언제 연습하니?
B: 운전할 때, 항상 영어 테이프를 들어.

Unit test

1.

1. Walking home
2. Having finished the test
3. (Being) Neglected by all
4. Turning to the left there
5. It being fine
6. Having seen her once before
7. Not receiving any answer
8. (Being) Unemployed

2.

1. When I was returning home or When I returned home
2. If you turn to the right
3. Though she had no money
4. When all things are considered
5. As she was tired out
6. Because I had received no answer from her.
7. Because she doesn't have a car

Writing Pattern Practice

1.

Taking a bath
Crossing the street

2

2.

Feeling very tired

Having no money

3.

Turning to the left

4.

Understanding what you say

5.

listening to the radio

6.

Getting dressed

7.

Not knowing what to do

Unit 43_ 분사구문의 의미상주어/ 부대상황

P.22

Dialogue

A: 네가 TV 안 봤으면 좋겠어.

B: 미안. 자려던 참이었어?

A: 응, TV가 켜있으면 잘 못자. 내일 아침에 중요한 회의가 있거든.

B: 알았어. 끌게.

Unit test

1.

1. Speaking of   2. Frankly speaking,

3. compared with   4. Judging from

5. Granted that

2.

1. turned   2. following

3. bandaged   4. closed

5. crossed

3.

1. She fell asleep with the lights on.

2. Don't speak with your mouth full

3. She came into the room with a smile on her face.

4. He is sleeping with his mouth open.

5. He's studying with the radio turned on.

Writing Pattern Practice

1.

Considering his age

Judging from his accent

Granted that you were drunk

Frankly speaking

Strictly speaking

Provided[or Providing] (that)

seeing (that)

2.

She walked along the street, with her hair waving in the wind.

She is singing, with her eyes closed.

Listen to it, with your mouth shut.

Don't speak with your mouth full.

He was standing, with his hands in his pockets.

She went into the room, with a hat on.

Unit 44_ 수동태

P.26

Dialogue

(쇼핑몰에서)

A: 누가 도와 드리고 있나요?

B: 아니오. 중간 사이즈로 흰색 긴 셔츠를 사고 싶은데요.

A: 여기 좋은 것이 있어요. 30% 세일이구요.

B: 잘됐네요.

Unit test

1.

1. *Hamlet* was written by Shakespeare.

2. The roof is being repaired by a friend of mine.

3. Spanish is spoken in Chile.

4. This house was built in 1980

5. Your life will be changed by this book.

6. Adam has been arrested by the police.

7. The papers were being prepared by the secretary then.

8. This car is driven by electricity.

9. Many accidents are caused by dangerous driving.

10. Three hundred people are going to be employed by the company.

2.

1. called   2. were built

3. have been analyzed   4. had been stolen
5. is being painted   6. was being followed
7. be told   8. have been done

Writing Pattern Practice

1.

English is spoken in Canada.
This room is cleaned everyday.

2.

Your car is being towed.
Alex is being punished.

3.

Were you invited to the party?
This table was made by my grandfather.

4.

The house was being painted.

5.

I have been promoted.
Adam has been arrested.

6.

The singer knew he had been forgotten.

7.

You'll be told soon.

8.

This report will have been done by tomorrow.

9.

Who's going to be fired?
Who's going to be invited?

Unit 45_ 그 밖 여러 가지 수동태

| P.30

Dialogue

A: 잠깐 실례해도 될까요?
B: 그럼요.
A: 2-3분 있다가 올게요.
B: 네. 천천히 하세요.

Unit test

1.

1. be done   2. be paid

3. be loved   4. waken up

2.

1. to   2. to   3. with   4. about   5. at
6. with   7. to

3.

1 Elvis Presley was born in 1935.
2. English is spoken in Canada.
3. Was this building built 100 years ago?

Writing Pattern Practice

1.

Let it be done.
Let this knife not be touched.

2.

This report must be finished by tomorrow.
You will be given $100.

3.

I'm glad to be invited to the party.
Most people like to be given presents.

4.

I hate being treated unfairly.
I don't like being told what to do.
Nobody likes being kept waiting.

5.

Eric is known to everybody in this town.
I'm satisfied with my new job.
I was surprised at the news.
I'm concerned about you.

Unit 46_ 주의해야할 수동태

| P.34

Dialogue

A: 멋진 스웨터네!
B: 그렇지! 할머니가 나를 위해 만들어주신 거야.
A: 정말? 바느질 솜씨 있으시다. 잘 어울리는데.
B: 고마워.

Unit test

1.

1. My baby is taken care of by Mary.
2. I was laughed at by David.

3. Professor Lee is looked up by Everybody.
4. I was given a present by Kevin / A present was given to me by Kevin.
5. The winner was given a prize / A prize was given to the winner.
6. This cake was made for Kate (by someone).
7. He is called a fool (by them).
8. He was made to stop smoking by the doctor.
9. It is said that he is a nice person. / He is said to be a nice person.
10. It was believed that the Earth was flat. / The Earth was believed to be flat.

2.

1. He was considered a genius.
2. He is called stupid.
3. Nothing was sent to me.
4. Stories were read to the children.

Writing Pattern Practice

1.

I was laughed at by everybody.
Sally's big nose is always made a fool of by me.
My baby is taken care of by Mary.

2.

I was given a present by Kevin.
This sweater was made for me.
A prize was given to the winner.
French is taught to us by Mrs. Lee.

3.

He is called a fool.
He was thought a great singer.
I was made to work overtime by my boss.
I have been made very happy.

4.

(It's said that~) It is said that he is honest.
(He is said~) He is said to be honest.
(It is expected that~) It is expected that the strike will end soon.
(The strike is expected~) The strike is expected to end soon.

Unit 47_ to부정사

P.38

Dialogue

A: 아, 저기 피자 먹고 싶어.
B: 들어가서 좀 먹자!
A: 아니야. 나 다이어트 중이란 말이야. 새해 결심을 작심삼일이 되게 하지는 않을래.
B: 살을 빼려면 규칙적으로 운동을 해야 할 것 같은데.

Unit test

1.

1. 명사   2. 부사   3. 명사   4. 부사
5. 부사   6. 형용사   7. 명사

2.

1. for   2. of   3. of   4. for   5. of

3.

1. Your handwriting is impossible to read.
2. I'm glad to have seen her.
3. I seem to have annoyed Ted.
4. It's nice to be having dinner with you.
5. Try not to be late.
6. It's important to listen to people.
7. I decided not to buy a used car.

Writing Pattern Practice

1.

It isn't easy to exercise everyday.
I love to meet people.

2.

Get me a chair to sit on.
I will get you something to drink.

3.

She ran to catch the bus.
This coffee is hot to drink.
To tell the truth, she is a stalker.

4.

I want to talk to(with) you.

5.

He seems to be studying in his room.

6.

I'm sorry to have kept you waiting.

I seem to have annoyed Mary yesterday.

7.
I tried not to bother my father.

8.
It's time for everybody to go to bed.
It's unusual for him to joke.
It was careless of you to say that.
It was sweet of you to remember my birthday.

Unit 48_동사+to부정사, 동사+목적어 +to부정사, 의문사+to부정사

P.42

Dialogue

A: 실례합니다. Main 가에 어떻게 가는지 말씀해 주시 겠어요?
B: 세 블록을 계속 가세요. 바로 거기에요.
A: 걷기에 먼가요?
B: 아니오, 걸어서 5분 거리에요.

Unit test

1.
1. where to park   2. how to get
3. who(m) to ask   4. when to leave
5. whether to meet

2.
1. I want to see the manager.
2. I hope to hear from you.
3. We didn't expect her to leave this early.
4. I want you to listen to me.
5. I don't know who to invite.
6. Tell me how to improve my pronunciation.
7. I don't know what to say.
8. I can't decide whether to answer her letter.

Writing Pattern Practice

1.
I want to go alone.
I hope to hear from you.
We expected to be late.
I'm planning to go to Europe.

2.
I want you to come to my birthday party.

I didn't expect her to come this early.
Who taught you to swim?
I asked Jane to be more careful.
I reminded my sister to buy coffee.
Who asked you to pay for the meal?

3.
I don't know what to eat.
Do you know how to use this machine?
I don't know who(m) to invite.
I can't decide whether to answer her letter.

Unit 49_ to부정사를 이용한 다양한 표현

P.45

Dialogue

A: 들어와. 다시 봐서 기쁘다.
B: 여기에 오게 되어서 기뻐.
A: 마실 것 한잔 줄까?
B: 물이면 돼.

Unit test

1.
1. to hear   2. to see
3. to call   4. to be
5. to rain   6. to drink

2.
1. I sat down so that I could rest.
2. I kept quiet so that I wouldn't bother my dad.

3.
1. She's so young that she can't get married.
2. The food was so hot that I/you/we couldn't eat.
3. They spoke so fast that we couldn't understand.

4.
1. Those apples are so ripe that I/you/we can eat.
2. She's so rich that she can buy a BMW.
3. He was so experienced that he could do the job.

5.
1. She's the last one to know the truth.
2. He's the last one to tell a lie.

Writing Pattern Practice

1.

It was nice to hear from you.
I was sorry to call so late.
You were lucky not to be fired.
It's likely to rain.
I'm willing to see you soon.
Are you ready to go out?

2.

Would you like something to drink?
Do you need something to write with?

3.

He came to New York (in order) to look for job.
We kept quiet (in order) not to bother her.

4.

I was too tired to go to work.
They spoke too fast for us to understand.

5.

Sally is old enough to see that movie.
Benny was experienced enough to do the job.

6.

Shiela is the last one to know the truth.
Tom is the last one to tell a lie.

Unit 50_ 동명사

| P.49

Dialogue

A: 뭐 하고 싶니? 영화 보는 것도 재미있을 것 같은데.
B: 물어봐줘서 고마운데, 그럴 기분이 아니야.
A: 가자. 나가는 게 너한테도 좋을 거야.
B: 아니야, 오늘밤은 집에 있고 싶어.

Unit test

1.

1. 분   2. 동   3. 동   4. 동   5. 분   6. 분
7. 동   8. 동   9. 분   10. 동

2.

1. 목   2. 주   3. 보   4. 전   5. 전   6.목
7. 목   8. 보   9. 주   10. 전

3.

1. Dose my smoking annoy you?

2. Do you mind me coming in?
3. The party was ruined by David's having to go home early.
4. I saw him getting on the bus.

Writing Pattern Practice

1.

Travelling is fun.
I enjoy travelling.
My hobby is travelling.
I feel like travelling.

2.

I'm ashamed of having been rude.
She admitted having broken the CD player.

3.

Would you mind not turning on the TV?
I'm proud of never having cheated before.

4.

Does my smoking annoy you?
I was upset about Sarah's trying to lie to me.

5.

Do you mind me coming in?
We're sure of the rumor being true.
I saw him getting off the bus.

6.

I feel like going for a walk.
Eating less is good for your health.
Thank you for waiting.

Unit 51_ 동사+동명사, 동사+목적어+ 동명사

| P.53

Dialogue

(극장에서)
A: 그 영화 보셨나요?
B: 예, 하지만 두 번 봐도 상관없어요.
A: 정말이예요?
B: 물론이죠. 다시 볼 만한 가치가 있는 영화거든요. 빨리 DVD가 나왔으면 좋겠어요.

정답 및 해설 **7**

Unit test

1.

avoid, can't help, put off, enjoy, suggest, mind, consider

2.

prefer, hate, begin, start, continue

3.

1. She suggested going to the zoo.
2. Would you mind passing the bread?
3. I can't imagine him dancing.
4. Nobody can stop him doing what he wants to.
5. It started raining again.
6. I forgot to lock the door.
7. He spent all his time sleeping.
8. He went on talking about his job.
9. This car needs servicing.
10. I stopped walking.

Writing Pattern Practice

1.

I enjoy cooking.
He has finished repairing his car.
My uncle has given up smoking.
I can't help falling in love with you.
The doctor suggested taking a long holiday.
You keep interrupting when I'm talking.

2.

I dislike people telling a lie.
I can't imagine him cooking.
My grandpa spends all his time gardening.
I saw him getting out of the car.
This treatment will prevent cancer from developing.

3.

I like walking(=to walk) in the rain.
It started raining(=to rain) again.

4.

I tried to finish it as quickly as I could.
Why don't we try pushing this car together?
I remember buying my first bicycle.
Remember to e-mail me.
I forgot to call Larry.
I will never forget meeting you.
Sally went on to talk about her other problems.
Cindy went on talking about her boyfriend for

hours.
You need to get more exercise.
This tire needs changing.
He deserves to get all As.
I don't think his article deserves reading.
I stopped to rest.
I stopped running.

Unit 52_ 동명사를 이용한 다양한 쓰임

| P.58

Dialogue

A: 오래간만이에요. 그동안 어떻게 지내셨어요?
B: 일하느라 바빴죠.
A: 새로운 일은 어때요?
B: 나쁘지 않아요. 적응하고 있어요.

Unit test

1.

1. is no	2. could not help
3. used to	4. What do you say
5. On	

2.

1. It is no use crying over spilt milk.
2. I couldn't help laughing.
3. I'm busy studying.
4. I feel like eating pizza.
5. Let's go dancing.
6. We look forward to hearing from you.
7. I object to your marrying Alice.
8. Did you have any trouble getting a visa?
9. This is worth reading.
10. Your shoes need mending.

Writing Pattern Practice

1.

There is no telling what will happen in the future.

2.

It is no use crying over spilt milk.
It is no use arguing about it.

3.

I couldn't help laughing.
I couldn't help wondering.

4.

I was busy cleaning.

The secretary is busy (in) answering phone calls.

5.

I feel like throwing up.

I feel like going out for dinner.

6.

Let's go hiking.

7.

I look forward to seeing you.

8.

I got used to living in Seoul.

I've got used to her being late.

9.

Do you object to working on Saturdays?

10.

I don't think they have trouble finding this place.

11.

France is worth visiting.

12.

What do you say to eating out?

13.

On seeing me, he ran away.

14.

You can't make an omelette without breaking eggs.

15.

My shoes need shining.

Your hair needs cutting.

REVIEW I

1.

1. surprised
2. tiring
3. shocked
4. bored
5. locked
6. parked
7. wearing
8. mashed
9. cut
10. Scrambled

2.

1. Feeling sleepy, I went to bed.

2. Being a foreigner, he needs to practice English.
3. Not knowing his phone number, I wasn't able to contact him.
4. Running out of money, we couldn't afford to travel to Europe.
5. Not getting here on time, they couldn't make it to the first class.

3.

1. Having saved some money, we bought a car.
2. Having taken a shower, she got dressed.

4.

1. Children are loved by everybody.
2. (Let) it be done.
3. Her son is being looked after by Sally.
4. (This cake) was made by my mother.
5. (I) was made to work overtime by my boss.

5.

1. of → for   2. of → for
3. for → of   4. to not → not to
5. coming → to come

6.

1. seeing   2. to call
3. moving   4. to drink
5. taking   6. to be
7. smoking

해설

1.

1,2. to부정사의 의미상 주어를 밝히는 경우, 보통 「for+목적격」형태를 to부정사 앞에 쓴다.
3. to부정사의 의미상 주어를 밝히는 경우, 사람의 성질을 나타내는 형용사가 사용되면「of+목적격」형태를 쓴다.
4. to부정사의 부정은「not+to부정사」형태를 쓴다.
5. 동사 expect는 '~가 …하기를 기대하다/예상하다' 라는 뜻일 경우「expect+목적어+to부정사」형태로 쓴다.

REVIEW 2

1. ③   **2.** ③

3. (with) her feet (in) the water

호주에는 많은 악어들이 있다. Elizabeth는 16살 소녀인데, 작은 강 옆에 앉아 있었다. 그녀는 발을 물에 담근 채로 쉬고 있었다. 갑자기, 3미터가 넘는 악어가 물 밖으로 점프해서 그녀를 죽이려 했다. 다행히도, 그녀는 나뭇가지 하나를 잡을 수 있었다. 그녀의 어머니는 어떤 일이 일어나고 있는지를 보고 물속으로 뛰어 들어갔다. 그녀는 Elizabeth를 안전하게 끌어당겼고 악어는 사라졌다.

4. ③

해석

당신은 아침식사를 하십니까? 많은 사람들은 바빠서 아침에 영양가 있는 아침식사를 못하고 있습니다. 만약 당신이 아침식사를 거른다면 당신은 사고하거나 일을 수행하는데 최선을 할 수 없을 것입니다. 많은 영양학자들은 아침식사가 하루 중 가장 중요한 식사라는데 동의합니다. 그러므로 아침식사로 높은 단백질과 높은 에너지의 식사를 하는 것은 중요합니다. 시간이 없더라도 아침 먹는 것을 잊지 마십시오. 아침마다 10분씩 일찍 일어나서 아침을 드세요.

06 | 문장 연결하기

Unit 53_ 시간 전치사

P.68

Dialogue

A: 메리 크리스마스!
B: 너도!
A: 크리스마스 날에 뭐 특별한 일 있니?
B: 아니, 그냥 집에 있을 것 같아.

Unit test

1.
1. on　2. on　3. X　4. X　5. in　6. at
7. on　8. X　9. in　10. in

2.
1. until　2. until　3. until　4. by　5. until
6. by　7. by　8. until　9. by　10. until

3.
1. during　2. for　3. in　4. through

Writing Pattern Practice

1.
I get up at 7 o'clock.
What do you usually do at Christmas?
I was born in July.
I'm leaving on May 1.
We have a meeting on Monday morning.

2.
We'll have to leave by this evening.
Can I stay until this weekend?

3.
I'll stay here for about a week.
We went to Hawaii during the summer vacation.
I've been busy all through the week.

4.
Brush your teeth before you go to bed.
We take a coffee break after lunch.
Ask me again in three or four days.
He'll be back within the next month.

5.
I've been here since 1999.
I work from 9 to 5.

Unit 54_ 장소 전치사

P.72

Dialogue

A: 이 버스 디즈니랜드 가요?
B: 아니오. 잘못 탔어요. 그린라인 버스를 탔어야 했어요. 다음 정거장에서 타시면 돼요.
A: 오래 걸리나요?
B: 그렇게 오래 걸리지 않아요.

Unit test

1.
1. in　2. out of　3. on　4. off　5. under
6. by

2.
1. to　2. across　3. for　4. down

Writing Pattern Practice

1.

What do you have in your pocket?
Get out of the car.

2.

Stop at the traffic light(s).
I lay (down) on the floor.
Take off your hat.

3.

Look at the bridge over the river.
He lifted his hands above his head.
A boat passed under the bridge.
The sun has already sunk below the horizon.

4.

She was sitting by the window.
Come and sit between Tom and Mary .
Look at the house among the trees.

5.

Are you from the United States?
I'm going to work.
Did he leave for Busan?

6.

The sun came up.
A man came down the stairs.

7.

He was walking along the street.
She lives across the river.
We passed through a tunnel.

Unit 55_ 전치사의 활용

P.77

Dialogue

A: 나는 이번 주말에 스키타러 가려고 해. 같이 갈래?
B: 나도 갈래. 나는 스키를 좋아하거든. 어디로?
A: 가장 가까운 용평 스키 리조트로 갈까 생각 중이야.
B: 좋아.

Unit test

1.

1. for   2. between   3. of   4. about   5. of

6. to   7. about   8. to   9. to   10. for
11. about   12. of

2.

1. Do you have a good relationship with your relatives?
2. Be kind to everybody.
3. She is mad about what you did.
4. What are they excited about?
5. Prices depend upon supply and demand.
6. You should be ashamed of yourself.
7. Why don't you apply for the job?
8. I'm proud of my son.

Writing Pattern Practice

1.

What was the cause of the accident?
There are some differences between you and me.
Do you have a good relationship with your parents?

2.

Be kind to everybody.
Are you mad at me?
Mary is angry about what you said to her.
I'm worried about his health.
What are you so nervous about?
I'm sick of eating the same food.
I'm proud of you.
She's married to a millionaire.

3.

I'm going to apply for the job.
Would you like a cup of coffee?
He complained of a headache.
Prices depend on(upon) supply and demand.
I dreamed about you last night.
I sometimes dream of being rich.
Did you hear about the fight in the restaurant?

Unit 56_ 동사구

P.81

Dialogue

(쇼핑몰에서)
A: 제게 너무 작네요, 그렇지 않아요?
B: 더 큰 걸로 사시면 되죠. 여기 있어요. 벗으시고 이

것으로 입어보세요.
A: 이것은 맞는데요. 얼마에요?
B: $25에요.

Unit test

1.
1. show up
2. put out
3. Look out
4. Wake up
5. pick, up

2.
1. Put, on
2. Take, off
3. Put on
4. went out
5. got out of
6. get on
7. got off
8. wake, up
9. fill out
10. pick, up
11. got in

3.
1. A new model came out.
2. The stain won't come out.
3. The sun came up.
4. Why didn't you wake me up?
5. Drop me off at the corner.

Writing Pattern Practice

Put on your glasses.
Take off your socks.
The plane is taking off.
He came in the room.
Brad Pitt came out in that movie.
We went out for dinner.
Get in the taxi.
She got out of the car.
I got on the bus.
We got off the train.
Wake up your sister.
Look out!
I'm going to see off my friend.
He didn't show up at the meeting.
Please put out your cigarette.
I'll pick him up.
Drop me off over there.
The meeting has been put off.
The button came off.
Throw them away.
The Civil War broke out in 1861.

Dialogue

A: 오늘밤 영화 보러 가는 게 어때?
B: 생각해 둔 특별한 영화가 있니?
A: 아니. 가서 뭐하나 보자.
B: 그러자. 8시에 데리러갈게.

Unit test

1.
1. and
2. but
3. and
4. nor
5. or
6. or
7. and
8. or
9. and
10. nor

2.
1. or
2. and
3. and
4. but
5. or
6. so

3.
1. Mary both speaks and writes Chinese.
2. He's in either Chicago or New York.
3. Sally is not only pretty but also clever.

Writing Pattern Practice

1.
I bought vegetables and milk.
Go and see what he's doing.
Come and see me.
Both Tom and Jane are from the United States.
Jack repairs both cars and motobikes.

2.
He's handsome but boring.
Not Cindy but you should come.
Not only Cindy but (also) you should come.

3.
Would you like coffee or tea?
Get up now, or you'll miss the bus.
Either Sarah or I am going to attend the meeting.
That's neither interesting nor true.
You are neither right nor wrong.

4.
He was late, so he hurried up.
I didn't have a watch, so I didn't know the time.

Unit 58_ 문장의 병렬구조

Dialogue

A: Monica! 막 저녁을 먹고 있었어. 좀 먹을래?
B: 괜찮아. 또 피자 먹어? 건강에 안 좋아.
A: 가끔 혼자 괜찮은 음식을 해먹어.
B: 즉석음식 먹지 말고 건강에 좋은 음식 먹으려고 노력해봐.

Unit test

1.
1. drank and danced
2. Either Mary or I
3. likes golf but hates tennis
4. He had a bad temper, but everybody liked him
5. neither like nor dislike
6. sleeping and snoring
7. coffee or tea
8. Neither Kate nor Sue
9. neither smokes nor drinks
10. not only plays the piano, but also the violin.

2.
1. I was hungry and tired.
2. I ate breakfast but didn't eat lunch.
3. Both David and Nick were tired of studying English.
4. He is either American or Canadian.
5. Neither Jenny nor Ann can come to the party.

Writing Pattern Practice

1.
I bought a shirt and pants.
I like both reading and sleeping.
He talked slowly but clearly.
Would you like coffee or tea?
Either Mary or I will go there.
I neither like nor dislike him.

2.
I like to ski and to skate.
People swim not only in summer but also in winter.

3.
We brought the food and they supplied the drink.
The two boys are alike in looks but they are different in personality.

4.
I have taught English in Seoul, (in) Busan, and (in) Daegu.
Charlie not only bought a new car, but also (bought) a new motorbike.
Erin not only plays the piano, but also the violin.

REVIEW 1

1.
1. on   2. in   3. at   4. by   5. out of   6. X
7. X   8. in   9. over   10. X   11. on
12. on   13. down   14. by   15. X   16. in
17. through   18. by   19. until   20. to

REVIEW 2

1.
1. at   2. about   3. between   4. for
5. with   6. of   7. to

2.
1. ○   2. Pick up me → Pick me up
3. ○   4. ○   5. Drop off me → Drop me off
6. ○   7. ○   8. nor → or   9. or → nor
10. but → or

해설
2.
5. 목적어가 있는 동사구(동사+부사)일 경우, 목적어가 명사일 때 동사구 사이에 오거나 동사구 뒤에 위치할 수 있지만 대명사일 때는 동사구 사이에 와야 한다.
8. 「either A or B」는 'A와 B 둘 중 하나' 의 뜻이다.
9. 「neither A nor B」는 'A와 B 둘 다 아닌' 의 뜻이다.
10. 둘 중 하나를 선택하는 경우는 접속사 or을 쓴다.

3. ②

4. ①

5. ②

6. ③

7. ①

집에 정원이 있나요? 한국의 몇몇 동네에서는 정원을 가지고 있습니다. 정원 한 쪽은 야채가 심어져 있을 거구요. 다른 한쪽은 꽃이 심어져 있을 겁니다. 사람들은 요즘 점점 더 건강에 대해 관심을 가집니다. 우리가 재배한 야채는 먹기에 좋습니다. 우리를 성장하게 하고 건강을 유지하기 위해 필요한 영양을 섭취하게 해줍니다. 어떤 야채는 땅위로 자라고 어떤 야채는 땅 아래로 자랍니다. 꽃 정원은 매우 아름답습니다. 꽃이 피면 잘라서 집에 어울리는 아름다운 꽃꽂이를 만들 수도 있습니다.

8-9

Hello Kitty를 많이 본 적이 있을 겁니다. Hello Kitty는 가장 유명한 만화에 나오는 고양이입니다. Sanrio 회사는 그녀를 세계 곳곳에서 유명하게 만들었습니다. 매우 예쁘고 작은 코가 있으며 보통 리본이나 꽃을 머리에 달고 다닙니다. 가방이나 옷 그리고 펜과 같은 Kitty그림이 그려져 있는 제품은 22,000가지가 넘습니다. 약 40 여개의 나라에서 판매되었습니다.아이들뿐만 아니라 어른들도 Hello Kitty 제품을 삽니다. Sanrio의 큰 성공은 전세계 20-30대 여성들의 흥미를 끄는 제품을 만들 수 있다는 능력에 있습니다. 왜 사람들이 Hello Kitty를 좋아한다고 생각하세요? 아마도 그것은 입이 없기 때문인 것 같습니다. 그래서 그녀가 행복해 보이지도 슬퍼보이지도 않는 것입니다. 사람들이 행복하면 그들은 그녀를 보고 그녀 역시 행복하다고 생각하고 그들이 우울할 때면 그녀 역시 우울하다고 생각합니다. 사람들은 그녀가 그들이 느끼는 것과 같이 느끼는 친구라고 생각합니다.

8. ②

9. ④

Chapter 07 | 복잡한 구조 이해하기

Unit 59_ that, whether, if로 시작하는 명사

| P.96

Dialogue

A: 창백해 보이는데. 괜찮아?
B: 별로. 오늘 몸이 안 좋고 약간 어지러워.
A: 심각한 게 아니었으면 좋겠다.

B: 날씨 때문인 것 같아. 후덥지근하잖아.

Unit test

1.
1. I heard ✓ you'd got a new job.
2. I believe ✓ this is your coat.
3. It's obvious ✓ he doesn't have enough money to buy that car.
4. The fact is ✓ she came here for money.
5. Tell me ✓ you love me.
6. The problem is ✓ she doesn't speak English well.
7. It is a fact ✓ smoking can cause cancer.
8. The point is ✓ you're skinny enough now.
9. I thought ✓ you'd get lost.
10. You knew ✓ I wouldn't forget your birthday.

2.
1. whether(if) she is single
2. whether(if) there is an ATM near here
3. whether(if) he has a lot of money
4. whether(if) Jane loves me
5. whether(if) you are coming to my birthday party
6. whether(if) I should move to a new house
7. whether(if) you can lend me some money
8. whether(if) you can help me with my homework

Writing Pattern Practice

1.
It is surprising that he is still single.
It is known to everybody that you're married.
I hope (that) you'll have a wonderful time.
I think (that) it's a good idea.
The problem is that your English is not so good.
The point is that money isn't everything.
The important thing is that you are happy.

2.
Whether he's rich (or not) isn't important.
Do you know whether the rumor is true (or not)?
The question is whether the man can be trusted (or not).
We can't decide whether we should stay or (we should) leave.

3.
I'm not sure if I'll have time.
I wonder if he'll win the game.

I don't know if it'll rain tomorrow.
I asked if she could lend me the money.

Unit 60_ 의문사로 시작하는 명사절

P.99

Dialogue

A: 와. 너 일본어 꽤 잘한다.
B: 고마워.
A: 누가 가르쳐 준건지 말해봐.
B: 사실, 2~3년 일본에서 살았었어.

Unit test

1.

1. Do you know why she didn't come?
2. When do you guess it happened?
3. I don't know what her pone number is.
4. Where do you suppose Tom is?
5. I know where she lives.
6. Tell me who can help me.
7. Who do you think he is?
8. I asked him how he went to the mall.
9. I wonder how old she is.
10. Who do you imagine stole the money?

2.

1. Who do you suppose will replace her?
2. What do you think he does?
3. What do you believe the answer is?
4. What do you guess I will do next?
5. Where do you think Tom is?

Writing Pattern Practice

1.

Who(m) she loves is the question.
I don't know what he did last night.
The question is where she is from.
I want to know what his name is.
He didn't tell me who he met.

2.

I want to know who can give me a ride.
I don't know what brought him here.
The question is who took the money.

3.

When do you think the movie starts?
Where do you guess she is?
When do you suppose the accident happened?

How do you suppose he got out of here?

4.

Who you think sent the present to you?
What do you guess is the answer?

Unit 61_ 형용사절의 쓰임과 종류

P.102

Dialogue

A: 어떤 좌석으로 드릴까요?
B: 가능하면 다리를 뻗을 수 있는 복도좌석으로 주세요.
A: 네, 비상구 옆 자리가 있네요. 여기 탑승권 있습니다.
B: 고맙습니다.

Unit test

1.

1. Have you got the book which(that) is really easy to read?
2. The movie which(that) Michael recommended to me was very good.
3. That's the man who(that) I really wanted to see.
4. I went to see Mr. and Mrs. Hart whose children I looked after a few years ago.
5. I have a vacuum cleaner which(that) you can use.
6. Britney Spears is a singer who(that) is very famous in the world.
7. I have something which(that) will clean that carpet.
8. This is the house which(that) has three bedrooms.
9. Where is that nurse who(m)(that) I saw last time?
10. She married a man who(m)(that) she met on a bus.

2.
1. X   2. X   5. X   6. X   7. X   9. X

Writing Pattern Practice

1.

I met a man who knows you.
Those are the people who live next door.
People who eat less live longer.
Sally is a person who(m) everybody loves.
Do you remember the people who(m) we met at

the meeting?

I saw a girl whose hair is blonde.

2.

Do you have a pen which I can use?

There's some bread which you might like.

That is a house which has three bedrooms.

3.

I like people that smile a lot.

Do you have anything that will clean this carpet?

The job that he got was boring.

Did you like the steak that we ate yesterday?

It's the best book that I've ever read.

All that I say is true.

Unit 62_ 관계대명사 what

P.106

Dialogue

A: 화면이 보이니?

B: 아니. 잘 안보여. 내 앞에 있는 남자가 너무 커.

A: 그럴 것 같았어. 나하고 자리 바꿀래?

B : 넌 참 이해심이 많구나. 고마워.

Unit test

1.

1. I can't believe what you said.
2. My sister gave me what I needed.
3. I didn't agree with what you explained to me.
4. This is what I have.
5. He showed me what he bought yesterday.
6. She lost what she owned.

2.

1. What I want is a place to sit down.
2. This is what Tome made.
3. I'm not what I used to be.
4. What she said made me angry.
5. I gave her what she needed.
6. What he needs is money.
7. What I want to know is his phone number.

Writing Pattern Practice

1.

What she said made me angry.

Money isn't what makes me happy.

He can give me what I need.

This is what Tom made.

This is what I wanted.

She lost what she owned.

What I want is a place to sit down.

What he needs is money.

What I want to know is his phone number.

I don't understand what you are talking about.

I know what you did last summer.

What I'm trying to say is that I love you.

2.

I'm not interested in what she has.

I'm not what I used to be.

Sally is attractive, and what is better, she is good-natured.

Nick is self-centered, and what is worse, he is dull.

Sam is, what is called, a Prince Charming.

Unit 63_ 관계부사

P.109

Dialogue

A: 속상해요. 나 너무 뚱뚱해. 다이어트를 해야 할 것 같아요.

B: 여보, 그럴 필요 없어요. 나는 지금 그대로의 당신이 좋아. 당신은 완벽해요.

Unit test

1.

1. where   2. why   3. X   4. how   5. when
6. why   7. where   8. X   9. when
10. where   11. why   12. X

2.

1. which I used to live in
2. why you left me
3. when we got married
4. how he did it

3.

1. I remember the house where I was born.
2. Do you know the reason why he stole the money?
3. This is the way I study English.
4. Do you remember the day when you first

came here?

Writing Pattern Practice

1.
This is the place where I first met him.
This is the pace where a school used to be.
I remember the house where I was born.

2.
Do you remember the day when we first met?
2002 was the year when we got married.
Sunday is the day when we go to church.

3.
I know the reason why she left you.
I can't tell you the reason why he was absent.
Do you know the reason why he stole the money?

4.
This is how he studies English.
I like the way she teaches.
How you passed the exam is a mystery.

Unit 64_ 제한적용법/ 계속적용법

P.113

Dialogue

A: 어려운 부탁 좀 들어줄래?
B: 물론, 뭔데?
A: Cindy는 California에서 온 사람인데, 아파트를 구하고 있어. 너는 전문가이니까 그녀를 좀 도와줄래?
B: 당연히 도와줘야지. 네 친구가 내 친구니까.

Unit test

1.
1. X who(that)
2. , who
3. , which
4. , who ,
5. , which
6. X which(that)
7. , which
8. , which

2.
1. David, who works with me, is quite funny.
2. He goes jogging everyday, which keeps him healthy.
3. I have a friend who lives in Italy.
4. She wrote a book on stress management,

which I recommend.
5. I went to Busan where I was born.
6. I went to Busan, where I stayed there for a month.

Writing Pattern Practice

1.
I had two friends who became cooks.
He had a daughter who became a singer.
I have a friend who lives in Italy.

2.
Cindy, who lives next door to Benny, is quite pretty.
Kate, who is my boss, is really boring.
He had a daughter, who became a singer.
Sarah said she was sick, which was a lie.
Grandpa ordered a pizza, which was a surprise to me.
He goes jogging everyday, which keeps him healthy.

3.
I went to Busan where I was born.
The place where we live is so beautiful.

4.
I went to Busan, where I stayed there for a month.
I stayed in Seattle, where I used to study there.

Unit 65_ 복합관계대명사/ 복합관계부사

P.117

Dialogue

A: 공포영화 빌렸는데 같이 볼래?
B: 좋아.
A: 로맨틱한 것도 하나 빌렸어.
B: 무서운 것으로 보자. 얼마든지 무서워도 상관없어. 얼마나 오래 하는데?
A: 대략 두 시간 반 정도.

Unit test

1.
1. 명   2. 부   3. 부   4. 명   5. 부   6. 부
7. 부   8. 명   9. 부   10. 부

2.

1. Whoever wants to pass the exam must study hard.
2. Choose whichever you want.
3. I'll give you whatever you need.
4. Whatever happens, keep calm.
5. Wherever you go, I will be with you.
6. Whenever you come, I'll be pleased.
7. However far it may be, you must go.
8. Give it to whomever you like.

Writing Pattern Practice

1.

Whoever wants to pass the exam must study hard.
Whoever may come to the party, I'll be glad.

2.

Give it to whomever you like.
Choose whichever you want.
I will give you whatever you need.
You can take whatever you like.

3.

A wizard can become whatever he wants.

4.

Whatever happens, I'm on your side.
Whichever you may choose, you'll be satisfied.
Whatever you did, I don't care about it.

5.

Wherever you go, you'll find Star Bucks.
However tired you may be, you must do it.
Whenever you come, I'll be pleased.

Unit 66_ 시간/ 조건의 부사절

| P.121

Dialogue

A: 샌드위치 하나 더 먹을래?
B: 고맙지만, 더 못 먹겠어.
A: 디저트는 먹을 거지, 그렇지?
B: 글쎄, 네가 먹는다면 나도 먹을게.

Unit test

1.

1. In case   2. unless   3. If   4. when
5. before   6. until   7. by the time

2.

1. c   2. d   3. b   4. a   5. e   6. f

3.

1. will rain → rains   2. will come → comes
3. will fall → falls   4. will have → have

해설

1.~5. 시간 부사절에서는 현재시제가 미래시제를 대신한다는 점을 유의한다.

Writing Pattern Practice

1.

Give me a call when he comes back.
As I was taking a shower, the phone rang.
You should brush your teeth before you go to bed.
While you were sleeping, Kate stopped by.
I'll visit you as soon as I arrive in Korea.
I don't care about money as long as you love me.
I'll be waiting here until he shows up.
Before he got married, he worked as a mechanic.
After she finished the school, she went to China.

2.

If you come, I'll be glad.
I'll be there unless it snows.
In case it rains, you should take your umbrella.
As far as I know, she is very nice.

Unit 67_ 이유/ 양보/ 결과의 부사절

| P.125

Dialogue

A: 이번 주 특별한 계획 있니?
B: 크리스마스 선물 사러 가야하는데.
A: 부럽다. 나는 이번 주말도 일해. 크리스마스가 얼마 안 남았지만.
B: 안됐네.

Unit test

1.
1. Although
2. so that
3. so, that
4. such, that
5. Because
6. though

2.
1. e   2. d   3. a   4. b   5. c

3.
1. Although he was bad-tempered he had lots of friends.
2. Since it was getting dark we had to go home.
3. He talked so quietly that we couldn't talk to him.
4. He is such a good student that he got a high score on the TOEIC test.

Writing Pattern Practice

1.

Because I was mad at him, I didn't want to talk to him.

Since it was getting dark, we had to go home.

Now that the finals are over, I can have fun with my friends.

2.

Though he is 8 years old, he speaks five languages.

I loved the story even though it was totally fictitious.

3.

I'll give you the key so that you can unlock the door.

Let's start now, so that we can have enough time.

4.

Susie is so kind that everybody likes her.

Susie is such a kind person that everybody likes her.

Unit 68_ 가정법

| P.129

Dialogue

A: 어젯밤 늦어서 미안해. 일 때문에 꼼짝도 못했어.

B: 나라면 그런 거짓말은 하지 않겠어요. 어제 밤 술 마신 것 알아요.
A: 이상한데. 왜 그렇게 말하는 거야?
B: Brad가 당신을 술집에서 봤대요.

Unit test

1.
1. have, will visit
2. will be, don't come
3. wash, will dry
4. help, will finish
5. see, will ask
6. will be, come
7. doesn't come, will go

3.
1. had, would
2. were, could
3. had done, have failed
4. had, would
5. should
6. eat, will/ can
7. were, would
8. were to, would

Writing Pattern Practice

1.

If you get here before eight, we can catch the train.

If you should run into Terry, tell him to call me.

If I were to be a student again, I would study music.

2.

If I were rich, I could buy that car.

If I were you, I wouldn't go there.

If I had a car, I could go to see you more often.

3.

If John had played well, the team would have won.

If I had known your phone number, I could have called you.

4.

If I had finished my report yesterday, I could hang out with my friends now.

Unit 69_ 가정법의 응용

| P.133

Dialogue

A: 갈 시간인 것 같은데.
B: 벌써? 커피 더 안 마실래?

A: 그리고 싶은데 내일 아침 일찍 일어나야 돼.
B: 그렇구나. 좀 더 있다가 가면 좋을 텐데.

Unit test

1.
1. I don't have a brother
2. I'm not in your shoes
3. I don't have enough time
4. she didn't come to the meeting.
5. I wasn't at the party.

2.
1. Why aren't you brushing your teeth?
2. Why aren't you getting up?
3. Why aren't you vacuuming the floor?

3.
1. unless   2. Suppose   3. Provided

Writing Pattern Practice

1.
I wish I could speak Spanish.
I wish I were in your shoes.

2.
I wish Jane had come to my birthday party yesterday.
I wish I had been there.

3.
He talks as if he were an old man.
He talked as if he were an old man.

4.
He talks as if he had seen a ghost.
He talked as if he had seen a ghost.

5.
It's time that you went to bed.

6.
Unless it rains,~
Provided(Providing) he doesn't come late,~
Suppose(Supposing) you picked up 10,000 dollars,~

REVIEW I

1. where were the President and his wife staying → where the President and his wife staying were
2. where did I live → where I lived
3. what time is it → what time it is
4. who was the most important person in our life → who the most important person in our life was
5. who did you call → who you called
6. how do you have such a good memory → how you have such a good memory
7. who are you → who you are
8. what time does the basketball game begin → what time the basketball game begins
9. if does he have a friend to count on → if he has a friend to count on
10. if could he lend me some money. → if he could lend me some money
11. which → who(that)
12. whose → which(that)
13. what → which(that) or 'the thing' 삭제
14. what → which(that) or 'the thing' 삭제
15. what → which(that) or 'the thing' 삭제

해설

1.~10. 의문문이 다른 문장 속에서 명사절로 쓰여 주어, 목적어, 보어 역할을 하는 것을 간접의문문이라고 한다. 이때 의문문의 「의문사+동사+주어」의 형태는 간접의문문에서 「의문사+주어+동사」형태로 바뀐다.

11. 선행사가 사람이고 주어역할을 할 때는 관계대명사 who나 that을 쓴다.

12. 선행사가 사람이 아니고 목적어역할을 할 때는 관계대명사 which나 that을 쓴다.

13. 14. 15. 관계대명사 what 앞에는 선행사(꾸밈을 받는 명사)를 쓰지 않는다.

2.
1. whom
2. what
3. which
4. which
5. X

3.
1. which
2. where
3. which
4. who
5. who(m)

6. who
7. whose
8. who
9. who(m)
10. who(m)

REVIEW 2

1. ④

2. ④

3. ③

4. ②

5. ④

6. ①

7. ④

8.
1. is
2. were
3. were
4. could be
5. had been
6. will buy
7. had known
8. would

9. ②

해석

여러분은 아마 Harry Potter 시리즈 중 하나를 보거나 읽었을 것이다. Harry Potter는 삼촌과 숙모와 함께 사는 고아였다. 그는 그의 삶 중 여러 해를 그를 싫어하는 가정의 계단 밑에서 잠을 자면서 지내왔다. Harry Potter는 여러 면에서 매우 평범하지 않은 소년이었다. 우선, 그는 다른 시간보다 여름방학을 제일 싫어했다. 또, 그는 그 자신이 마법사라는 것을 알게 되었다! 하루는 Harry의 생일날, 그는 편지를 받았다. 그 후로 100통의 편지가 Harry에게 보내졌는데 그것들은 모두 Hogwart's 마법사 학교에서 공부하라는 초대장이었다. 그것에는 "우리는 당신이 Hogwarts School of Witchcraft and Wizardry에 합격된 것을 알려드리게 되어서 기쁩니다."라고 쓰여 있었다. Harry는 그 초대를 받아들였고 그의 삼촌과 숙모를 떠났다.이것이 J.K. Rowling의 매력적이고 재미있는 첫 데뷔작 Harry Potter에서 Harry Potter에게 일어나는 일이다. 더 알고 싶으면 책을 읽거나 영화를 봐야할 것이다.

Chapter 08 | 주의해야할 용법

Unit 70_ 시제일치

| P.142

Dialogue

A: 스포츠를 잘 하시나 봐요.
B: 네. 스포츠를 매우 좋아하죠. 당신은 요?
A: 격렬한 운동은 좋아하지 않아요. 배드민턴을 쳤었는데 지금은 서툴러요.
B: 좋아요. 언제 배드민턴이나 치러가죠?

Unit test

1.
1. she had a cold
2. Kelly had finished her lunch
3. he would give up
4. water is made up of hydrogen and oxygen

2.
1. <u>may</u> → might
2. <u>breaks</u> → broke
3. <u>made</u> → makes
4. <u>got</u> → gets
5. <u>will</u> → would

해설
1. 5. 주절의 시제가 과거, 과거완료시제일 경우, 종속절에는 과거나 과거완료동사를 쓴다.
2. 역사적인 사실일 경우 항상 과거시제로만 쓴다.
3. 속담, 격언 등은 보통 현재시제로 쓴다.
4. 반복적인 행위를 말하는 경우 현재시제로 쓴다.

3.
1. has breakfast
2. were sick in bed
3. broke out
4. goes around
5. comes home

Writing Pattern Practice

1.
Sally now lives in New York.
David and I went dancing last night.

2.

I know (that) you need some money.

I know (that) you needed some money.

I know (that) you'll need some money.

3.

I thought (that) you were sick in bed.

I thought (that) you had been sick in bed.

4.

The boy learned that light travels faster than sound.

Brian said that he always exercises in the morning.

5.

We know (that) Caesar was the first Roman emperor.

6.

If my brother comes back home, I'll give him a big hug.

Unit 71_ 화법

| P.146

Dialogue

(파티에서)

A: Judy! 와줘서 고마워. 못 온다고 한줄 알았는데.

B: 그랬었는데. 회의가 연기됐어.

A: 잘됐다. 와서 앉아. 뭐 좀 마실래?

B: 응, 오렌지 주스 줘.

Unit test

1.

1. Laura said (that) she didn't like vegetables.
2. David said (that) he was really hungry.
3. Tom said (that) he woke up feeling sick, so he stayed in bed.
4. Nick told me (that) he had to go them.
5. I asked the girl where she lived.
6. David asked if that was my bag.
7. My boss told me to finish my report the next day.
8. Captain Kim ordered(=commanded) private Lee not to move.

2.

1. you weren't going out.
2. English wasn't difficult
3. you weren't leaving for Tokyo
4. that restaurant wasn't expensive
5. David didn't like you

Writing Pattern Practice

1.

Nick said (that) he had to go then.

Jack told me (that) my brother didn't go there.

2.

I asked the girl what she was eating.

I asked the police officer where the nearest bank was.

David asked whether(=if) that was my pen.

The boy asked whether(=if) I had seen a dinosaur.

3.

My mother told me to clean my room.

Sam invited me to go to his birthday party.

Vicky asked me to close the window.

Unit 72_ 강조, 도치

| P.150

Dialogue

A: 저기 David과 Ann 간다.

B: 나는 왜 David이 Ann과 사귀는지 모르겠어.

A: 나도 그래. 그녀는 잘난 척하고 자기가 무엇이나 다 아는 것처럼 말하는데.

B: David은 그녀의 무엇을 보는 걸까?

Unit test

1.

1. He did lie to me.
2. What on earth are you talking about?
3. Who in the world broke into the house?
4. It was I that met Kate at the cafe
5. It was Kate that I met at the cafe.
6. It was at the cafe that I met Kate.

2.

1. Here comes your mother.
2. There goes the taxi.

3. There it goes.
4. Never have I seen a ghost.

3.
1. So do I.
2. Neither can I.
3. So am I.
4. Neither have I.
5. So must I.

Writing Pattern Practice

1.
I do love you.
John does hate sports.
He did attend the meeting.

2.
Where on earth are you going?
Who in the world stole the money?

3.
It was yesterday that I saw him.
It's coffee that I want.
It's not you that I love.
It wasn't Judy that I saw.
It wasn't in Germany that I met her.

4.
Here comes your sister.
There goes the bus.
Here she comes.
There it goes.

5.
Never have I been this nervous.

6.
So am I.
So was I.
Neither have I.

Unit 73_ 생략
| P.154

Dialogue

A: 괜찮으면 네 차 좀 썼으면 좋겠는데.
B: 글쎄, 언제까지?
A: 이달 말까지.
B: 잘 모르겠네. 생각해봐야할 것 같아.

Unit test

1.
1. the best singer ever
2. he was
3. it is
4. speak English
5. she was

2.
1. is allowed
2. I am
3. served first

3.
1. See you later
2. No pains, no gains
3. Hands off

Writing Pattern Practice

1.
I met George and had dinner with him.
Yes, he was.
I don't sing as well as you.
No, but I'm going to.
Just do as I told you to.

2.
I'll give you the money today if necessary.
I'd like to borrow this book if possible.
Though rich, he's not happy at all.

3.
No smoking!
No parking!
No pains, no gains!
Hands off!
First come, first served.

Unit 74_ 부정표현
| P.157

Dialogue

A: Jess는 어때? 그를 아직 만나?
B: 아니, 우리는 헤어졌어.
A: 왜?
B: 우리는 공통점이 거의 없어. 처음에 내가 왜 그에게 반했는지 모르겠어.

Unit test

1.
1. rarely
2. completely
3. no longer
4. nothing but
5. not, until

2.
1. Cactuses need little water.
2. Nancy drinks little coffee.
3. Few people understand his ideas.
4. There is little water in that bottle.
5. I can hardly see it.
6. I can scarcely recognize who he is.
7. The rich are not always happy.
8. She did nothing but cry.
9. Cindy is no longer staying in this city.
10. He didn't stop watching TV until his mother got angry.

Writing Pattern Practice

1.
There were few passengers in the bus.
We had very little snow last year.

2.
He hardly smiles.
I can barely hear you.
My mother rarely speaks ill of others.

3.
The rich are not always happy.
Heather isn't always kind to us.
Not both of you can get the chance.
I didn't completely understand what he was saying.

4.
Age is nothing but a number.
He didn't stop walking until it got dark.
This ring is no longer any meaning to me.

Unit 75_ 1, 2, 3형식

P.160

Dialogue

A: 그 옷을 입으니까 정말 멋져 보인다.

B: 고마워. 그 드레스도 너에게 잘 어울리는데.
A: 응, 고마워. 너무 화려한 게 아닌 가 약간 걱정 했었어.
B: 전혀 안 그래. 걱정하지 마.

Unit test

1.
1. 1형식
2. 2형식
3. 3형식
4. 3형식
5. 2형식
6. 1형식
7. 3형식
8. 1형식
9. 2형식
10. 1형식
11. 3형식
12. 1형식
13. 2형식
14. 2형식
15. 1형식

2.
1. funny
2. gorgeous
3. what I wanted
4. true
5. to find the way to the station
6. that you have no money
7. that Jane is going out with Nick

3.
1. working
2. to go for a walk
3. what to buy for Cindy
4. it will rain.
5. that she was fascinating.
6. if I could do anything to help.
7. what you were trying to say.

Writing Pattern Practice

1.
I write to my mother once a month.
A nice convertible suddenly appeared when I walked down the street.
There are a lot of people at the bank.
There is some misunderstanding between us.
There is something you have to know.

24

2.

Do I sound strange today?

The problem is that you don't have enough money to study abroad.

The fact is that I know nothing about it.

3.

Most people drink too much soda.

Who owns the car which is parked outside?

We don't allow smoking in the lecture room.

I wonder who to invite.

I feel sorry that I lost my temper this morning.

I wonder if you could lend me some money.

I want to know why he told me a lie.

Unit 76_ 4, 5형식

| P.164

Dialogue

A: 왜 그렇게 우울해보여? 나쁜 일 있니?

B: 나는 우쭐대는 사람들과 일하는데 신물이나.

A: 나도 그래. 항상 잘난 척하는 사람들은 짜증나더라.

B: 맞아.

Unit test

1.

1. 4형식
2. 5형식
3. 5형식
4. 5형식
5. 5형식
6. 4형식
7. 5형식
8. 5형식
9. 5형식
10. 4형식
11. 5형식
12. 4형식
13. 4형식
14. 5형식
15. 4형식
16. 4형식

2.

1. to → for
2. for → to
3. do → to do
4. cutting → cut

5. felt → feel

해설

1. buy, get, make, find, choose 등의 동사가 쓰인 경우, 4형식문장을 3형식문장으로 바꿀 때는 「주어+동사+직접목적어+for+간접목적어」의 형태로 한다.

2. give, show, tell, offer 등의 동사가 쓰인 경우, 4형식문장을 3형식문장으로 바꿀 때는 「주어+동사+직접목적어+to+간접목적어」의 형태로 한다.

3. 「would like+목적어+to부정사」는 '~가 …하기를 바란다' 라는 뜻이다.

4. 목적어 my hair와 목적보어 cut의 관계가 수동이므로 목적보어자리에는 과거분사가 와야 한다.

5. 「make+목적어+동사원형/형용사」는 '~가 …하도록 만든다' 라는 뜻이다.

3.

1. What makes you so happy?
2. I'd like my hair dyed.
3. I told you not to be late.
4. Would you like me to go?
5. Who left the door open?

Writing Pattern Practice

1.

He showed me the way to the bank.

She asked me a favor.

2.

He offered a drink to me.

Give it back to me.

3.

Will you find a good one for me?

4.

You can call me whatever you want.

Who named you Bob?

5.

What makes you so embarrassed?

I want my hair cut.

She pushed the door shut.

6.

How many times do I have to tell you not to be late?

I want you to fill out the form.

7.

I want to make my girlfriend feel happy today.
Let me know if you have a question.

REVIEW 1

1.
1. makes
2. might
3. play
4. see
5. were

2.
1. (David told me that) he was a college student.
2. (He told me that) he lived on his own and worked two jobs.
3. (He told me that) he'd been always busy making money for two years.
4. (He told me that) he thought he could go to Italy to study music the next year.

3.
1. I did pass
2. She does seem to be crying.
3. Do come in.
4. Where on earth have you been?
5. Why in the world did she marry Sam?
6. It was John that ate spaghetti for lunch at TGIF's.
7. It was spaghetti that John ate for lunch at TGIF's.
8. It was at TGIF's that John ate spaghetti for lunch
9. Here comes the bus.
10. Never have I seen such a good player.

REVIEW 2

1. ④

2. ③

3. ①

4. ③

5. ②

6. ④

7. ④

8. ①

9. ③

10. ⑤

11. ②

12. ⑤

13. ③

14. ⑤

15-17

해석

안녕, Jack!
어떻게 지내요? 저요? 보통 때처럼 열심히 일하고 있죠. 피곤하긴 하지만. Sally와 나는 휴가를 기다리고 있어요. 휴가동안에 뭐 할 거예요? 우리는 일주일동안 강원도에 캠핑 가는 게 좋을 것 같다고 생각했는데.
당신이 관심 있는지 궁금해요. 관심 있다면 알려줘요. 그리고 날짜나 다른 것들을 의논하죠. Sally가 당신과 당신 부인과 같이 가는 게 좋겠다고 하더군요. 작년에 제주도에서 재미있었잖아요. 기억나요? 곧 뵙기를 바래요.

David
추신. 멋진 주말 고마웠어요. 정말 재미있었어요. 혹시 집에 제 재킷을 두고 왔나요? 그렇다면 보내 줄 수 있을까요?

15. ②

16. (Sally said to me,) "It will be good to get together with him and his wife."

17. ①

해석

토마토는 오랫동안 건강식품으로 여겨져 왔다. 토마토에 대해서 여러분이 알아야할 중요한 점이 있다. 의사는 한 주에 열 스푼의 토마토소스를 먹기를 추천한다. "토마토 속에는 리코펜이라는 성분이 있다." 라고 말한다. 이 성분은 굉장한 효과가 있다. 그는 "토마토소스나 케첩을 먹는 것이 그냥 토마토를 먹는 것에 비해 더 좋다. 여러분의 장기에 더욱 흡수되도록 하는데 도움을 준다." 라고 말한다.